These Are the Times That Try Men's Souls

These Are the Times That Try Men's Souls

America — Then and Now in the Words of Tom Paine

Edited by John Armor

Illustrated by Olga Calco

Paine, Thomas, 1737-1809.

These are the times that try men's souls : America-- then and now in the words of Tom Paine / edited by John Armor ; illustrated by Olga Calco. -- Alexandria, VA : American Civil Rights Union, c2010.

p. ; cm.

ISBN: 978-145753-514-7
Includes biographical references and index.

1. United States--Politics and government--1775-1783. 2. United States--Politics and government--1783-1809. 3. United States--Politics and government--21st century. I. Armor, John C. (d. 2010). II. Title. III. Title: America-- then and now in the words of Tom Paine.

JC177.A4 A76 2010
320.51/2092--dc22 1009

Published by
The American Civil Rights Union
3213 Duke Street, #625
Alexandria, VA 22314
www.theacru.org

In association with
Dog Ear Publishing
4011 Vincennes Rd.
Indianapolis, IN 46268
www.DogEarPublishing.net

Manufactured in the United States of America

Thomas Paine
1737-1809

WITHOUT the pen of Paine
The sword of Washington
Would have been wielded in vain.

–John Adams, widely attributed,
likely suggested by Joel Barlow,
American diplomat

THE author . . . is unconnected with any party,
And under no sort of influence public or private,
But the influence of reason and principle.

–Tom Paine, February 14, 1776

DEDICATED to all
who gave the last full measure for America,
beginning with Crispus Attucks at the
Boston Massacre, March 5, 1770.

Table of Contents

Foreword

YOU HAVE IN your hands a remarkable digital book that represents more than a decade's work by one of America's most astute legal scholars.

It's not only a fresh look at one of our country's most important Founders, but it's a joy to read. We have forgotten how great a debt we owe to Tom Paine, known best as the "pamphleteer of the Revolution."

It was with words like the following that he rallied millions of Americans to the cause of liberty:

"These are the times that try men's souls.
The summer soldier and the sunshine patriot will,
In this crisis, shrink from the service of their country;
But he that stands it now, deserves the love and thanks of
Man and woman.
Tyranny, like hell, is not easily conquered;
Yet we have this consolation with us,
That the harder the conflict, the more glorious the triumph.
What we obtain too cheap, we esteem too lightly."

John Armor, who died just before this book's initial release in 2010, has left us with a precious gift—a unique compilation of the best of Tom Paine's writings along with his own witty and profound comments that help us understand the context.

John was not only a prolific writer and defender of constitutionalism, but was a very colorful man. Some people remember him as a wonderful Ben Franklin impersonator, who brought that Founding Father's words to life in his full-costumed appearances at Tea Party rallies and other events.

Tucked away in the North Carolina mountains, John wielded a mighty pen for freedom. He reminded us constantly of our God-given rights and why they are enshrined in the Constitution.

When the ACRU unveiled These Are the Times at "An Evening with Tom Paine" in October 2010, I was honored to make a few remarks. Click here for the video.

We are living in an age when the courts have strayed far from first principles and wandered off into a "Living Constitution." That was Justice John Brennan's description, and I'd have to say it's misleading; that poisonous liberal doctrine is more about burying and replacing the Constitution than in breathing new life into it. John Armor, who liked to get right to the point, might have put it even less delicately.

John was a thorn in the side of the American Civil Liberties Union, which he exposed with ACLU Outrage columns regularly on the American Civil Rights Union's website. His wit can be found in those dispatches, and in the words he wrote in the margins of this very well organized book.

I think Tom Paine would be proud that his work was honored so well by a modern master like John.

Edwin Meese III

Edwin Meese III
Washington, D.C.

Introduction

THOMAS PAINE left school at thirteen and apprenticed to his father, an English corset-maker. He died at age seventy-two in America, penniless, reviled by some, forgotten by most, and was buried in at least two different graves. Between his inauspicious beginning and his tragic end, he wrote the words that created the United States of America from thirteen squabbling colonies.

Others claimed independence for America. Others fought its war of independence. Others created its government and served in it. But it was Paine who turned mere colonists into Americans, into citizens of a new nation.

He was self-taught in the classics of his day. Those books showed him the power of the English tongue. Franklin and others taught him the nature of the people. From those two wellsprings, he crafted the words that defined the times, the crises, and the nation in the bestselling book written by an American—a slim volume called *Common Sense*. One copy of this book was sold for every two Americans who could read. No book other than the Bible has ever matched that feat.

America has never faced a greater crisis than it did after July 1776; the existence of the nation hung in the balance. Others had said the price of freedom was war: none stated the cause as well as Paine.

Almost all of the one-third of Americans who could read did read his words. Almost all the others heard them read in taverns and public meetings across the nation. George Washington had Paine's words read to the remnants of his oft-defeated army just before they crossed the Delaware in a snowstorm to defeat the Hessians in Trenton on the day after Christmas, 1776. This comment, attributed to John Adams and likely suggested by American diplomat Joel Barlow, is simple truth, not hyperbole: "Without the pen of Paine, the sword of Washington would have been wielded in vain."

Two centuries of living the American experiment in self-government have proved that some words are timeless. Since 1776, America has faced many crises, two of which threatened its very existence as a nation. Those two were the War of 1812 and the Civil War. Other crises have placed its citizens' lives or the principles of its freedom in grave danger.

Paine peered deeply into the heart of America, when only a handful of rebels were contemplating the creation of a nation like this. Paine saw clearly the nature of the threat and the sacrifices necessary to prevail. He wrote about these with such conviction that citizens of Pennsylvania, Virginia, and the other colonies knew for the first time that in truth they were all Americans. Paine was the first person to write the words "United States of America." His words taught all citizens that they had a common cause with one another. He showed citizens what Ben Franklin said to Congress on the signing of the Declaration of Independence: "We must hang together, or assuredly we will hang separately."

This book has three distinct purposes. The first is to present Paine's words as he wrote them. No other editor has discovered that Paine wrote not in mere prose, but in blank verse. But that is what he did.

The second purpose is related to the first. The best of writing becomes timeless. It is not bound by time and circumstance. So, the second purpose is to connect Paine's concepts from the founding of America to the crises this nation faces now.

The third purpose is to explain the technique of Tom Paine. The power of his words is not accidental. The sources he studied and the way he wrote are facts that can be shown, and more importantly, can be learned. So, Paine's writings are an object lesson to all writers who seek to write with excellence. It is not by accident that Strunk and

White, in their classic *The Elements of Style*, chose a line by Paine as the perfect English sentence.

This book was written for more than just the history, then and now. Paine learned great writing by reading great writers. Great writing means knowledge, skill, and passion. All three elements must be present. So, this book is also intended for writers who aspire to write like Tom Paine. It shows how he accomplished what he did.

To begin the study of Paine, he must be set in the context of his times. There is abundant proof that Americans originally thought of themselves as citizens of the nations of Delaware, Rhode Island, and the other eleven colonies. The Constitutional Convention in 1787 nearly broke apart in failure over whether the states in Congress would have equal representation or representation based on population. Gunning Bedford, delegate from Delaware, shocked the other delegates by suggesting that the smaller states "will find some foreign ally of more honor and good faith, who will take them by the hand and do them justice" if they did not retain their equal power in Congress. Rhode Island not only refused to attend the convention, it refused to hold a convention to ratify the Constitution. Not until Congress threatened to exchange ambassadors with Rhode Island and tax the import of its products into America did that state relent, conduct its ratification, and rejoin the United States of America.

Thinking like this was quite common among the citizens of the various colonies that would become states. Then Tom Paine wrote *Common Sense*, and later *The American Crisis*, published first in chapter form in newspapers. His great achievement was to cause Americans to think of themselves as Americans.

There are no key distinctions between crises then and crises now. Differences between sailing ships and airplanes, between mail post riders and the Internet, do not define the essence of threats to America. In all the crises that America has faced, faces now, and will face in the future, there are these common threads: we must know as a people the task that we confront, the freedoms we will lose if we fail to act and act together, and then we must take such steps and make such sacrifices as the cause demands. It was exactly this sort of analysis that Paine lead us through, beginning in 1776.

As a man, Paine made more enemies than friends. He also had a tendency to turn his friends into enemies. But as a philosopher, his vision was clear and sure. He saw the essence of America and taught it to men and women who had never dreamed of that. He taught the basics of leadership and citizenship, qualities which become essential in times of crisis.

It is the fortunate nature of America to call forth men of talent in times of need. Never has this nature been more important than when a self-taught English writer arrived in America and turned up in Philadelphia with a letter of introduction to Benjamin Franklin's son-in-law, Richard Bache. Franklin had met Paine through a mutual friend who attended science lectures in London with Paine. Paine was quite ill when he reached Philadelphia, and his life was saved by Dr. John Kearsley, another Franklin friend. Through a series of introductions, Paine ultimately found what he sought—a chance to write, edit, and publish his work.

This book gathers the most powerful statements of Tom Paine, puts them in the context of his era, and offers parallels that show their relevance to our times. It also explains why his words remain enduring and haunting, clear and strong, centuries after they were written.

The four greatest sources of quotations in modern English are the King James Version of the Bible and the works of Shakespeare, Alexander Pope, and Miguel Cervantes' *Don Quixote*. These are written entirely, or in part, in the "heroic measure," which in Shakespeare and Pope became iambic pentameter. Ideas expressed in this poetic form are unique in their power and their imprint on human memory. From reading these sources, Paine learned to write.

Despite leaving school early, Paine was introduced to Homer's works, *The Iliad* and *The Odyssey*. These were the earliest works created in heroic measure. For their initial centuries, these epic poems were not written down—they were spoken, memorized, and passed down orally.

The style in which Paine wrote was ideally suited to be read aloud in public, which was exactly how most Americans received his words.

The three greatest crises in American history were the American Revolution, the War of 1812, and the Civil War. Only these events threatened the life of America. Paine's words were the equal of the era that called them forth, which depended on his words. Others since then have drawn from the same well. Francis Scott Key was a student of the classics. He wrote these words after the critical battle of the War of 1812, the defense of Fort McHenry:

"O, say can you see, by the dawn's early light,
What so proudly we hailed at the twilight's last gleaming. . . ."

Abraham Lincoln was also a student of the classics. He wrote these words after the critical battle of the Civil War, when he dedicated the graveyard at Gettysburg, Pennsylvania:

". . . Government of the people, by the people, and for the people
Shall not perish from the earth."

Great leadership demands great language. Others in other nations have used the same, classic language. In the depths of World War II, Winston Churchill said,

"If the British Empire and its Commonwealth
last for a thousand years, men will still say,
'This was their finest hour.'"

In the founding documents of America, the same influences are evident. Jefferson wrote this in the Declaration of Independence:

"All men are endowed by their Creator
With certain unalienable rights—
That among these are life, liberty, and the pursuit of happiness."

Randall Thompson wrote a choral work based on a text by Thomas Jefferson. The title of his piece is "The Testament of Freedom." Its second movement's opening lines show that this style of writing is memorable in part because it is musical:

"We have counted the cost of this contest,
And find nothing so dreadful as voluntary slavery. . . ."

Jefferson, Madison, Franklin, and Washington are remembered as Founders or Framers. Even Patrick Henry, whose contribution was eloquent but slight, is better known than Paine. Tom Paine is truly "the forgotten Framer." He was never elected to any government post, except in the French Republic. And his candid statements in the French Assembly nearly sent him to the guillotine. Paine played no part in writing the Declaration, the Constitution, or any laws of this nation. And yet, without Paine's words, there would be no America.

The editor of this book is John C. Armor, a First Amendment lawyer who has practiced in the U.S. Supreme Court. The illustrator is Olga A. Calco, a Russian-born and -trained artist, who now lives in the United States with her husband and children. Many thoughtful people have encouraged and contributed to the creation of this book. Most important has been the commitment of Susan Carleson, the CEO of the American Civil Rights Union. Her decision that this book deserved to be published made it so.

Special thanks are due to Olga Calco. Almost a decade ago, I decided this book must have excellent illustrations. She met that requirement. I also thank my editor, Doug Schneider, who took great care with this project. Initial design work was done excellently by Claire Liston. Final layout and typesetting was done with patience by Kelly Cole. Ilan Wurman is the most able text reader I have ever worked with. And without my wife's understanding that I would be buried in obscure books for months at a time, this book could not have come to fruition.

These Are the Times That Try Men's Souls is all I hoped it could be. It became that way only because of the unique help of these individuals.

It is once again worthwhile to review the life and times of Tom Paine and draw strength and purpose from his words, because it is once again true that:

"These are the times that try men's souls."

Highlands, North Carolina
November 2009

Editor's Note

THERE are two words used by Paine throughout his writings with the English spellings which are changed here to the American spellings: "independence" and "defence." The only other major change is reducing Paine's extreme use of words in all capital letters and italics for emphasis. Italics have been retained where necessary to the meaning of the passage. Capitalization is in accord with modern English.

Words like "honour," whose English spelling is sometimes seen in America, have been left untouched. Paine's common use of "s" for "z" in words like "organised" and "civilised" has been changed to standard American English.

The other change in Paine's originals is to change his obsolete use of "it's" for the possessive pronoun, rather than "its." Today, this substitution is among the most common made by English writers.

Because Paine's works were widely pirated, there are many variations in his texts. The best available Internet and printed versions shown in the bibliography were used in preparing this book.

Ellipses (. . .) indicate the instances where some words from Paine's writing have been removed. The instances where a word or letter was added are indicated with brackets [ ].

The table of citations from Paine's works is on page 235.

"These
are
the times
that try
men's
souls..."

Canto I:
On the American Crisis

THESE are the times that try men's souls.
The summer soldier and the sunshine patriot will,
In this crisis, shrink from the service of their country;
But he that stands it now, deserves the love and thanks of
man and woman.
Tyranny, like hell, is not easily conquered;
Yet we have this consolation with us,
That the harder the conflict, the more glorious the triumph.
What we obtain too cheap, we esteem too lightly:
It is dearness only that gives every thing its value.
Heaven knows how to put a proper price upon its goods;
And it would be strange indeed if so celestial an article
As freedom should not be highly rated.
Britain, with an army to enforce her tyranny,
Has declared that she has a right (not only to tax)
But "to bind us in all cases whatsoever,"
And if being bound in that manner, is not slavery,
Then is there not such a thing as slavery upon earth.
Even the expression is impious;
For so unlimited a power can belong only to God.

AC-I-91

It is equally wrong to avoid war when it is necessary as it is to seek war when it is not. In every American crisis involving the force of war, the decision must be made by Congress, not merely by the president, for only then is that our decision as the Constitution intends.

Bring the doctrine of reconciliation to the touchstone of
nature,
And then tell me, whether you can hereafter
Love, honour, and faithfully serve the power

Paine's words influenced not only his fellow citizens, but the leaders of the American Revolution. Compare this with Samuel Adams' later and more famous quotation which ends, "Crouch down and lick the hands which feed you. May your chains set lightly upon you, and may posterity forget that ye were our countrymen!"

That hath carried fire and sword into your land?
If you cannot do all these, then are you only
Deceiving yourselves, and by your delay bringing ruin upon posterity.
Your future connection with Britain, whom you can neither love nor honour,
Will be forced and unnatural, and being formed only on the plan
Of present convenience, will in a little time fall
Into a relapse more wretched than the first.
But if you say, you can still pass the violations over,
Then I ask, Hath your house been burnt?
Hath your property been destroyed before your face?
Are your wife and children destitute of a bed to lie on,
Or bread to live on? Have you lost a parent or a child
By their hands, and yourself the ruined and wretched survivor?
If you have not, then are you not a judge of those who have.
But if you have, and still can shake hands with the murderers,
Then you are unworthy of the name of husband, father, friend, or lover,
And whatever may be your rank or title in life,
You have the heart of a coward, and the spirit of a sycophant.
CS-143

It is the good fortune of many
To live distant from the scene of sorrow;
The evil is not sufficiently brought to their doors
To make them feel the precariousness . . . of all American[s] . . .
That seat of wretchedness will teach us wisdom,
And instruct us for ever to renounce a power
In whom we can have no trust.
CS-142

Every quiet method for peace hath been ineffectual.
Our prayers have been rejected with disdain;
And only tended to convince us, that nothing flatters vanity,
Or confirms obstinacy in Kings more than repeated
petitioning—

CS-144

The United States is today dealing with certain nations led by tyrants equal in arbitrary political power to King George III. Those tyrants possess powers of destruction that no king ever dreamt of. Are we making the same type of mistake—in dealing with the likes of North Korea, Syria, and Iran—that some Americans urged in dealing with King George III?

At a crisis, big, like the present, with expectation and events,
The whole country is called to unanimity and exertion.
Not an ability ought now to sleep, that can
Produce but a mite to the general good, nor even
A whisper to pass that militates against it.
The necessity of the case, and the importance of the
consequences,
Admit no delay from a friend, no apology from an enemy.
To spare now, would be the height of extravagance, and
To consult present ease, would be to sacrifice it perhaps
forever.

AC-IX-233

Let it be told to the future world, that in the depth of
winter,
When nothing but hope and virtue could survive,
That the city and the country, alarmed at one common
danger,
Came forth to meet and to repulse it. Say not
That thousands are gone, turn out your tens of thousands;
Throw not the burden of the day upon Providence,
But "show your faith by your works," that God may bless
you.
It matters not where you live, or what rank of life you hold,
The evil or the blessing will reach you all.
The far and the near, the home counties and the back,
The rich and the poor, will suffer or rejoice alike.

The first truth of any national crisis is: all Americans are threatened, so all must share in the necessary burdens of our defense. It is a simple truth that is often forgotten when times are easy and no threats are obvious.

The heart that feels not now is dead;
The blood of his children will curse his cowardice,
Who shrinks back at a time when a little
Might have saved the whole, and made them happy.
I love the man that can smile in trouble,
That can gather strength from distress, and grow brave
By reflection. 'Tis the business of little minds to shrink;
But he whose heart is firm, and whose conscience
Approves his conduct, will pursue his principles unto death.
My own line of reasoning is to myself as straight and clear
As a ray of light. Not all the treasures of the world,
So far as I believe, could have induced me to support
An offensive war, for I think it murder;
But if a thief breaks into my house,
Burns and destroys my property, and kills
Or threatens to kill me, or those that are in it,
And to "bind me in all cases whatsoever"
To his absolute will, am I to suffer it?
What signifies it to me, whether he who does it
Is a king or a common man; my countryman or not my countryman;
Whether it be done by an individual villain, or an army of them?
If we reason to the root of things we shall find no difference;
Neither can any just cause be assigned
Why we should punish in the one case and pardon in the other.
Let them call me rebel and welcome, I feel no concern from it;
But I should suffer the misery of devils, were I
To make a whore of my soul by swearing allegiance
To one whose character is that of a sottish, stupid,
Stubborn, worthless, brutish man.
I conceive likewise a horrid idea in receiving mercy

From a being, who at the last day shall be shrieking
To the rocks and mountains to cover him,
And fleeing with terror from the orphan, the widow,
And the slain of America.
There are cases which cannot be overdone by language,
And this is one. There are persons, too, who see not
The full extent of the evil which threatens them;
They solace themselves with hopes that the enemy,
If he succeed, will be merciful.
It is the madness of folly, to expect mercy
From those who have refused to do justice;
And even mercy, where conquest is the object, is only
A trick of war; the cunning of the fox is as murderous
As the violence of the wolf, and we ought to guard
  equally
Against both. Howe's first object is, partly by threats
And partly by promises, to terrify or seduce the people
To deliver up their arms and receive mercy.
The ministry recommended the same plan to Gage,
And this is what the Tories call making their peace,
"A peace which passeth all understanding" indeed!
A peace which would be the immediate forerunner
Of a worse ruin than any we have yet thought of.
Ye men of Pennsylvania, do reason upon these things!
Were the back counties to give up their arms,
They would fall an easy prey to the Indians,
Who are all armed: this perhaps is what
Some Tories would not be sorry for.
Were the home counties to deliver up their arms,
They would be exposed to the resentment of the back
  counties
Who would then have it in their power
To chastise their defection at pleasure.
And were any one state to give up its arms,

Here, Paine shows that he understands the non-military tricks of war far better than modern generals and presidents. Today's leaders should have a better understanding, since they have two centuries more of experience with international deception.

That state must be garrisoned by all Howe's army
Of Britons and Hessians to preserve it from the anger of
the rest.
Mutual fear is the principal link in the chain of mutual love,
And woe be to that state that breaks the compact.
Howe is mercifully inviting you to barbarous destruction,
And men must be either rogues or fools that will not see it.
I dwell not upon the vapors of imagination;
I bring reason to your ears, and,
In language as plain as A, B, C,
Hold up truth to your eyes.
AC-I-96

"Of more worth is
one honest man
To society and in
the eyes of God, than
All the crowned ruffians
who ever lived."

Canto II: On Tyranny

Tyranny is tyranny, regardless of its pretense. Paine wrote when the world was replete with kings. Logically, there are no important differences between those who are born into power and those who shoot their way into power or gain power by demagoguery and deception.

OF more worth is one honest man
To society and in the eyes of God
Than all the crowned ruffians that ever lived.

CS-135

The Heathens paid divine honours to their deceased kings,
And the Christian world hath improved on the plan
By doing the same to their living ones. How impious
Is the title of sacred majesty applied to a worm,
Who in the midst of his splendor is crumbling into dust!

CS-126

In short, monarchy and succession have laid
(Not this or that kingdom only) but the world
In blood and ashes. 'Tis a form of government which
The word of God bears testimony against, and blood will
attend it.

CS-134

But there is a truth that ought to be made known:
I have had the opportunity of seeing it; which is,
That notwithstanding appearances, there is not any
description of men
That despise monarchy so much as courtiers.
But they well know, that if it were seen by others,
As it is seen by them, the juggle could not be kept up;

Keeping in mind that the claim to power by kings is older, but not better, than those who seize power on their own, look at the men who surround modern tyrants. Except in the clothes they wear and titles they bear, are they any different from courtiers immemorial?

They are in the condition of men who get their living by a show,
And to whom the folly of that show is so familiar
That they ridicule it; but were the audience to be made
As wise in this respect as themselves, there would be
An end to the show and the profits with it.
The difference between a republican and a courtier
With respect to monarchy, is that the one opposes monarchy,
Believing it to be something; and the other
Laughs at it, knowing it to be nothing.
RM-I-488

This is supposing the present race of kings
In the world to have had an honourable origin;
Whereas it is more than probable, that could we
Take off the dark covering of antiquity,
And trace them to their first rise,
That we should find the first of them nothing better
Than the principal ruffian of some restless gang,
Whose savage manners or pre-eminence in subtility
Obtained him the title of chief among plunderers;
And who by increasing in power, and extending
His depredations, over-awed the quiet and defenseless
To purchase their safety by frequent contributions.
CS-130

When despotism has established itself for ages in a country,
As in France, it is not in the person of the king only that it resides.
It has the appearance of being so in show, and in nominal authority;
But it is not so in practice and in fact. It has its standard everywhere.

Every office and department has its despotism,
Founded upon custom and usage. Every place
Has its Bastille, and every Bastille its despot.
The original hereditary despotism . . . in the person of the king,
Divides and sub-divides itself into a thousand shapes and forms,
Till at last the whole of it is acted by deputation.
This was the case in France; and against this species
Of despotism, proceeding on through an endless labyrinth
Of office till the source of it is scarcely perceptible,
There is no mode of redress. It strengthens itself
By assuming the appearance of duty,
And tyrannizes under the pretense of obeying.

RM-I-444

Acceptance of tyranny can become a habit; subjugation can assume the false guise of duty. Paine understood, centuries before she wrote it, what Hannah Arendt meant by "the banality of evil."

What is called monarchy, always appears to me
A silly, contemptible thing. I compare it to something
Kept behind a curtain, about which there is a great deal
Of bustle and fuss, and a wonderful air of seeming solemnity;
But when, by any accident, the curtain happens
To be open—and the company see what it is,
They burst into laughter.

RM-II-569

Compare this with the classic scene in The Wizard of Oz. *Toto pulls back the curtain and the Wizard's image in flame and smoke bellows, "Pay no attention to the man behind the curtain." Recall that the Wizard was that rarest of creatures—a benevolent dictator with not an ounce of malice in him. Did Frank Baum read Paine before he wrote his book about the Land of Oz?*

It could have been no difficult thing in the early
And solitary ages of the world, while the chief employment
Of men was that of attending flocks and herds,
For a banditti of ruffians to overrun a country,
And lay it under contributions. Their power being thus established,
The chief of the band contrived to lose the name of
Robber in that of Monarch;
And hence the origin of Monarchy and Kings . . .

Neither poverty nor despair is the cause of war. The world has always had an ample supply of both, in different degree, in all its nations. Wars are always begun by governments, and not in equal measure by all types of governments. It is the tyrants of our day, like kings of Paine's day, who invite rebellion by their deeds and spark wars by their designs on their neighbors. This pattern will continue until all such governments have fallen in favor of republics at the will of the people. The maturation of the human race has already taken two centuries more than Paine imagined. The task is not done; the blood price remains to be paid. "They that take the sword shall perish with the sword" (Matthew 26:52).

Those bands of robbers having parceled out the world,
And divided it into dominions, began, as is naturally the case,
To quarrel with each other.
What at first was obtained by violence
Was considered by others as lawful to be taken,
And a second plunderer succeeded the first.
They alternately invaded the dominions which each had assigned
To himself, and the brutality with which they treated each other
Explains the original character of monarchy.
It was ruffian torturing ruffian.
The conqueror considered the conquered, not as his prisoner,
But his property. He led him in triumph rattling in chains,
And doomed him, at pleasure, to slavery or death.
As time obliterated the history of their beginning,
Their successors assumed new appearances,
To cut off the entail of their disgrace,
But their principles and objects remained the same.
What at first was plunder, assumed the softer name of revenue;
And the power originally usurped, they affected to inherit.
From such beginning of governments, what could be expected
But a continued system of war and extortion?
It has established itself into a trade.
The vice is not peculiar to one more than to another,
But is the common principle of all.
There does not exist within such governments
Sufficient stamina whereon to engraft reformation;
And the shortest . . . remedy is to begin anew on the ground of the nation.
What scenes of horror, what perfection of iniquity,

Present themselves in contemplating the character
And reviewing the history of such governments!
If we would delineate human nature with a baseness of heart
And hypocrisy of countenance that reflection would shudder at
And humanity disown, it is kings, courts and cabinets
That must sit for the portrait.
Man, naturally as he is, with all his faults
About him, is not up to the character.
Can we possibly suppose that if governments had originated
In a right principle, and had not an interest in pursuing a wrong one,
The world could have been in the wretched and quarrelsome
Condition we have seen it? What inducement
Has the farmer, while following the plough,
To lay aside his peaceful pursuit, and go
To war with the farmer of another country?
Or what inducement has the manufacturer?
What is dominion to them, or to any class of men in a nation?
Does it add an acre to any man's estate, or raise its value?
Are not conquest and defeat each of the same price,
And taxes the never-failing consequence?
—Though this reasoning may be good to a nation,
It is not so to a government.
War is the Pharo-table of governments,
And nations the dupes of the game.
If there is anything to wonder at in this miserable scene
Of governments more than might be expected,
It is the progress which the peaceful arts of agriculture, manufacture

Paine echoes Rousseau's idea that in their natural state, men are virtuous and benign; this is an exaggeration. But, Paine is right that governments, not individuals, are usually the causes of war.

And commerce have made beneath such a long
accumulating load
Of discouragement and oppression. It serves to show
That instinct in animals does not act with stronger impulse
Than the principles of society and civilization operate in
man.
Under all discouragements, he pursues his object,
And yields to nothing but impossibilities.
RM-II-II-556

All hereditary government is in its nature tyranny.
An heritable crown, or an heritable throne,
Or by what other fanciful name such things
May be called, have no other significant explanation
Than that mankind are heritable property.
To inherit a government, is to inherit the people,
As if they were flocks and herds.
RM-II-III-559

More of the citizens fell in this struggle than of their
opponents:
But four or five persons were seized by the populace,
And instantly put to death; the Governor of the Bastille,
And the Mayor of Paris, who was detected in the act
Of betraying them; and afterwards Foulon,
One of the new ministry, and Berthier, his son-in-law,
Who had accepted the office of intendant of Paris.
Their heads were stuck upon spikes, and carried about the
city;
And it is upon this mode of punishment that Mr. Burke
Builds a great part of his tragic scene.
Let us therefore examine how men came by the idea
Of punishing in this manner. They learn it from the
governments

They live under; and retaliate the punishments
They have been accustomed to behold.
The heads stuck upon spikes, which
Remained for years upon Temple Bar,
Differed nothing in the horror of the scene from those
Carried about upon spikes at Paris;
Yet this was done by the English Government.
It may perhaps be said that it signifies nothing to a man
What is done to him after he is dead;
But it signifies much to the living; it either
Tortures their feelings or hardens their hearts,
And in either case it instructs them
How to punish when power falls into their hands.
Lay then the axe to the root, and teach governments
humanity.
It is their sanguinary punishments which corrupt mankind.
In England the punishment in certain cases is by hanging,
Drawing and quartering; the heart of the sufferer is cut out
And held up to the view of the populace. In France,
Under the former Government, the punishments were not
less barbarous.
Who does not remember the execution of Damien,
Torn to pieces by horses? The effect of those cruel spectacles
Exhibited to the populace is to destroy tenderness or
excite revenge;
And by the base and false idea of governing men by terror,
Instead of reason, they become precedents.
It is over the lowest class of mankind that government
By terror is intended to operate, and it is on them
That it operates to the worst effect. They have
Sense enough to feel they are the objects aimed at;
And they inflict in their turn the examples of terror
They have been instructed to practice.

RM-I-453

Here Paine was replying to an attack on the French Revolution whose supporters beheaded some royalist leaders and paraded through Paris with their heads on pikes. Of course these were barbarous actions, but Paine would not condemn them. Instead, he defended them by saying that both the French and English governments had inflicted similar punishments in the past, and "taught" the French to do the same. This is "moral equivalency" two centuries before that phrase was invented.

But there is another and greater distinction for which no truly natural
Or religious reason can be assigned, and that is,
The distinction of men into KINGS and SUBJECTS.
Male and female are the distinctions of nature,
Good and bad the distinctions of heaven;
But how a race of men came into the world
So exalted above the rest, and distinguished like some new species,
Is worth enquiring into, and whether they are
The means of happiness or of misery to mankind.
CS-125

I cannot see on what grounds the king of Britain
Can look up to heaven for help against us:
A common murderer, a highwayman, or
A house-breaker, has as good a pretense as he.
AC-I-92

Tyrannies are always disguised in show and pageant. They are defended with slogans. The tyrant is deified; otherwise, the truth will bring them down. The "cult of personality" was not an accident in the Soviet Union, in China, or in many other nations. It is always a necessary ingredient of tyranny.

Some writers have explained the English constitution thus;
The king, say they, is one, the people another;
The peers are an house in behalf of the king;
The commons in behalf of the people;
But this hath all the distinctions of an house divided against itself;
And though the expressions be pleasantly arranged,
Yet when examined they appear idle and ambiguous;
And it will always happen, that the nicest construction that words
Are capable of, when applied to the description of some thing
Which either cannot exist, or is too incomprehensible
To be within the compass of description, will be
Words of sound only, and though they may amuse the ear,

They cannot inform the mind, for this explanation
includes
A previous question, viz. How came the king by a power
Which the people are afraid to trust, and always obliged to
check?
Such a power could not be the gift of a wise people,
Neither can any power, which needs checking,
Be from God; yet the provision, which
The constitution makes, supposes such a power to exist.
CS-122

That the crown is this overbearing part in the English
constitution
Needs not be mentioned, and that it derives its whole
consequence
Merely from being the giver of places and pensions
Is self-evident; wherefore, though we have been wise
enough
To shut and lock a door against absolute monarchy,
We at the same time have been foolish enough
To put the crown in possession of the key.
The prejudice of Englishmen, in favor
Of their own government by king, lords and commons,
Arises as much or more from national pride than reason.
Individuals are undoubtedly safer in England
Than in some other countries, but the will of the king
Is as much the law of the land in Britain as in France,
With this difference, that instead of proceeding directly
from his mouth,
It is handed to the people under the more formidable shape
Of an act of parliament. For the fate of Charles the First,
Hath only made kings more subtle—not more just.
Wherefore, laying aside all national pride and prejudice
In favor of modes and forms, the plain truth is,

"Being the giver of places and pensions" is the key to survival for all tyrants. Look to see who profits from a Saddam Hussein or a Fidel Castro and you will understand how and why they remain in power so long.

That it is wholly owing to the constitution of the people,
And not to the constitution of the government
That the crown is not as oppressive in England as in Turkey.
CS-123

Are tyranny, idiocy, and insanity confined to monarchs? Modern dictators display all these, especially the first, for a taste for tyranny is in all who force their way into office. Not that modern America is free of the tendency to elect idiots, but at least we need suffer them in office no more than four years, or six in the case of the United States Senate.

. . . When we see that nature acts as if she disowned
And sported with the hereditary system; that the mental character
Of successors, in all countries, is below the average of human understanding;
That one is a tyrant, another an idiot, a third insane,
And some all three together, it is impossible to attach
Confidence to it, when reason in man has power to act . . .
Would we make any office hereditary that
Required wisdom and abilities to fill it?
And where wisdom and abilities are not necessary,
Such an office, whatever it may be, is superfluous or insignificant. . . .
It requires some talents to be a common mechanic;
But to be a king requires only the animal figure of man—
A sort of breathing automaton.
RM-II-III-560

There never did, there never will, and there never can, exist a Parliament,
Or any description of men, or any generation of men,
In any country, possessed of the right or the power
Of binding and controlling posterity to the "end of time,"
Or of commanding for ever how the world shall be governed,
Or who shall govern it; and therefore all such clauses,
Acts or declarations by which the makers of them
Attempt to do what they have neither the right nor the power

To do, nor the power to execute, are in themselves null and void.
Every age and generation must be as free to act
For itself in all cases as the age and generations
Which preceded it. The vanity and presumption of governing
Beyond the grave is the most ridiculous and insolent of all tyrannies.
Man has no property in man; neither has any generation
A property in the generations which are to follow.
The Parliament or the people of 1688, or of any other period,
Had no more right to dispose of the people
Of the present day, or to bind or to control them
In any shape whatever, than the parliament or the people
Of the present day have to dispose of, bind or control
Those who are to live a hundred or a thousand years hence.
Every generation is, and must be,
Competent to all the purposes which its occasions require.
It is the living, and not the dead, that are to be accommodated.
When man ceases to be, his power and his wants cease with him;
And having no longer any participation in the concerns
Of this world, he has no longer any authority
In directing who shall be its governors, or how its government
Shall be organized, or how administered.

RM-I-438

The only way that a constitution laid down by men now dead is still valid is with provisions for amendment. That way, the law remains if the people choose not to change it. But that right to change it belongs only to the people, not to the legislature, the courts, or the president.

Absolute governments (tho' the disgrace of human nature)
Have this advantage with them, that they are simple;
If the people suffer, they know the head from which

Accurately placing the blame for failure is the necessary first step in curing a public problem. The very complexity of some modern programs, such as public education, hides the blame, so failure persists from generation to generation.

Their suffering springs, know likewise the remedy,
And are not bewildered by a variety of causes and cures.
But the constitution of England is so exceedingly complex,
That the nation may suffer for years together without being
Able to discover in which part the fault lies,
Some will say in one and some in another,
And every political physician will advise a different
medicine.
CS-120

Paine here describes what Jefferson called a "natural aristocracy" of merit, that those with skills to offer would arise as needed and the nation would take advantage of their gifts, each in their own way. Perhaps the three greatest demonstrations of this are the military, medicine, and the world of letters. Neither generals, doctors, nor writers are usually the children of the same. Nor do their own children necessarily succeed in their professions. Each of them achieve on their own merits, by and large.

Experience, in all ages, and in all countries,
Has demonstrated that it is impossible
To control Nature in her distribution of mental powers.
She gives them as she pleases.
Whatever is the rule by which she, apparently to us,
Scatters them among mankind, that rule remains a secret
To man. It would be as ridiculous to attempt to fix
The hereditaryship of human beauty, as of wisdom.
Whatever wisdom constituently is,
It is like a seedless plant;
It may be reared when it appears,
But it cannot be voluntarily produced.
There is always a sufficiency somewhere
In the general mass of society for all purposes;
But with respect to the parts of society,
It is continually changing its place.
RM-II-III-562

O ye that love mankind! Ye that dare oppose,
Not only the tyranny, but the tyrant, stand forth!
Every spot of the old world is overrun with oppression.
Freedom hath been hunted round the globe.
Asia, and Africa, have long expelled her—
Europe regards her like a stranger, and England

Hath given her warning to depart.
O! Receive the fugitive, and prepare in time an asylum for mankind.

CS-154

"Society in every state is a blessing,
But government even in its best state
Is but a necessary evil:
In its worst state, an intolerable one..."

Canto III: On Republican Government

SOCIETY in every state is a blessing,
But government even in its best state is but a necessary evil;
In its worst state, an intolerable one;
For when we suffer, or are exposed
To the same miseries by a government,
Which we might expect in a country without government,
Our calamity is heightened [since] we
Furnish the means by which we suffer!
Government, like dress, is the badge of lost innocence;
The palaces of kings are built on the ruins of the bowers
 of paradise.
For were the impulses of conscience clear, uniform, and
 irresistibly obeyed,
Man would need no other lawgiver;
But that not being the case, he finds it necessary
To surrender up a part of his property to furnish
Means for the protection of the rest;
And this he is induced to do by the same prudence
Which in every other case advises him
Out of two evils to choose the least.
Wherefore, security being the true design
And end of government, it unanswerably follows
That whatever form thereof appears most likely
To ensure it to us, with the least expense
And greatest benefit, is preferable to all others.

Compare Jefferson's words, written six months later, in the Declaration of Independence: "It is the Right of the People to alter or abolish it, and to institute new Government, laying its Foundation on such Principles . . . as to them shall seem most likely to effect their Safety and Happiness."

The Constitution guarantees to every state a "Republican form of Government." Unfortunately, many politicians—and some judges—have forgotten what that means and why it is important.

What is called a republic is not any particular form
Of government. It is wholly characteristical of the purport,
Matter or object for which government ought to be
Instituted, and on which it is to be employed,
res-publica, the public affairs, or the public good;
Or, literally translated, the public thing.
It is a word of a good original, referring to what ought
To be the character and business of government;
And in this sense it is naturally opposed to the word monarchy,
Which has a base original signification.
It means arbitrary power in an individual person;
In the exercise of which, himself, and not the *res-publica*, is the object.
Every government that does not act on the principle of a Republic,
Or in other words, that does not make the *res-publica*
Its whole and sole object, is not a good government.
Republican government is no other than
Government established and conducted
For the interest of the public, as well individually as collectively.
It is not necessarily connected with any particular form,
But it most naturally associates with the representative form,
As being best calculated to secure the end
For which a nation is at the expense of supporting it.
RM-II-III-565

Hitherto we have spoken only (and that but in part)
Of the natural rights of man. We have now
To consider the civil rights of man, and to show
How the one originates from the other.
Man did not enter into society to become worse than he was before,

Nor to have fewer rights than he had before,
But to have those rights better secured.
His natural rights are the foundation of all his civil rights.
But in order to pursue this distinction with more precision,
It will be necessary to mark the different
Qualities of natural and civil rights.
A few words will explain this. Natural rights
Are those which appertain to man in right of his existence.
Of this kind are all the intellectual rights, or
Rights of the mind, and also all those rights
Of acting as an individual for his own comfort and
happiness,
Which are not injurious to the natural rights of others.
Civil rights are those which appertain to man
In right of his being a member of society.
Every civil right has for its foundation some natural right
Pre-existing in the individual, but to the enjoyment of
which
His individual power is not, in all cases, sufficiently
competent.
Of this kind are all those which relate to security and
protection.
From this short review it will be easy to distinguish
Between that class of natural rights which man retains
After entering into society and
Those which he throws into the common stock
As a member of society. The natural rights which he retains
Are all those in which the Power to execute is as perfect
In the individual as the right itself. Among this class,
As is before mentioned, are all the intellectual rights,
Or rights of the mind; consequently religion is one of
those rights.
The natural rights which are not retained, are all those
In which, though the right is perfect in the individual,

It is an entirely separate question what rights individuals might have through a constitution and what rights they claim merely through political power. Individuals are no more just when they seize rights because they can than leaders are to seize power because they can. Reason illustrates the difference.

The power to execute them is defective. They
Answer not his purpose. A man, by natural right,
Has a right to judge in his own cause; and so far as
The right of the mind is concerned, he never surrenders it.
But what availeth it him to judge, if he has not power
To redress? He therefore deposits this right in the common stock
Of society, and takes the arm of society, of which
He is a part, in preference and in addition to his own.
Society grants him nothing. Every man is
A proprietor in society, and draws on the capital as a matter of right.
RM-I-464

It is not just the people within a nation who keep a tyrant in power. The world community also helps by playing along with the pretense that every tin-pot dictator with blood on his hands is entitled to equal respect as a "national leader." The main problem with the United Nations is that a majority of its voting members are iron-clad tyrannies. Living by the principles of its charter is therefore completely impossible.

Perhaps the disorders which threatened, or seemed to threaten,
On the decease of a leader and the choice of a new one
(For elections among ruffians could not be very orderly)
Induced many at first to favor hereditary pretensions;
By which means it happened, as it hath happened since,
That what at first was submitted to as a convenience,
Was afterwards claimed as a right. England, since the conquest,
Hath known some few good monarchs,
But groaned beneath a much larger number of bad ones;
Yet no man in his senses can say that their claim
Under William the Conqueror is a very honourable one.
A French bastard landing with an armed banditti,
And establishing himself king of England against the consent
Of the natives, is in plain terms a very paltry rascally original—
It certainly hath no divinity in it.
However, it is needless to spend much time

In exposing the folly of hereditary right,
If there are any so weak as to believe it,
Let them promiscuously worship the ass and lion, and
welcome.
I shall neither copy their humility, nor disturb their
devotion.

CS-131

The present time, likewise, is that peculiar time,
Which never happens to a nation but once,
Viz. the time of forming itself into a government.
Most nations have let slip the opportunity,
And . . . have been compelled to receive laws from their
conquerors,
Instead of making laws for themselves.
First, they had a king, and then a form of government;
Whereas, the articles or charter of government,
Should be formed first, and men delegated
To execute them afterwards: but from the errors
Of other nations, let us learn wisdom,
And lay hold of the present opportunity—
To begin government at the right end.

CS-163

There never has been, and never will be, a republican government without a constitution which limits the powers of the government. The critical questions are: who draws that constitution? And, how does that constitution provide for its own survival?

Thus necessity, like a gravitating power, would soon form
Our newly arrived emigrants into society,
The reciprocal blessing of which, would supersede,
And render the obligations of law and government
unnecessary
While they remained perfectly just to each other;
But as nothing but heaven is impregnable to vice,
It will unavoidably happen, that in proportion
As they surmount the first difficulties of emigration,
Which bound them together in a common cause,

Governments should act on specific issues where societies fail. But this is entirely different from thinking that any government can be a successful substitute for society.

They will begin to relax in their duty and attachment to each other;
And this remissness, will point out the necessity, of establishing
Some form of government to supply the defect of moral virtue.
CS-119

It is of interest that a proposal was before Congress to make three-fifths the required majority for the purpose of raising taxes on the citizens. Also, among the 1,000 amendments ever proposed in Congress to reform the manner of electing our presidents, one would have chosen them by lot from among the retiring senators, another would have done the same among sitting governors. Query whether we would have been better served in recent decades by those combined, than the quadrennial dog-and-pony show by which we now choose our presidents.

Let the assemblies be annual, with a President only.
The representation more equal. Their business wholly domestic,
And subject to the authority of a Continental Congress.
Let each colony be divided into six, eight, or ten,
Convenient districts, each district to send
A proper number of delegates to Congress,
So that each colony send at least thirty.
The whole number in Congress will be least 390.
Each Congress to sit and to choose a president by the following method.
When the delegates are met, let a colony be taken
From the whole thirteen colonies by lot, after which,
Let the whole Congress choose (by ballot)
A president from out of the delegates of *that* province.
. . . So proceeding on till the whole thirteen shall have had their proper rotation.
And in order that nothing may pass into a law
But what is satisfactorily just, not less than
Three fifths of the Congress to be called a majority.
He that will promote discord, under a government so equally formed as this,
Would have joined Lucifer in his revolt.
CS-150

Above then is the origin and rise of government;
Namely, a mode rendered necessary by the inability
Of moral virtue to govern the world;
Here too is the design and end of government,
Viz. freedom and security. And however our eyes
May be dazzled with snow, or our ears deceived by sound;
However prejudice may warp our wills, or interest
Darken our understanding, the simple voice
Of nature and of reason will say, it is right.
I draw my idea of the form of government from
A principle in nature, which no art can overturn,
Viz. that the more simple any thing is,
The less liable it is to be disordered,
And the easier repaired when disordered;
And with this maxim in view, I offer a few remarks
On the so much boasted constitution of England.
That it was noble for the dark and slavish times
In which it was erected, is granted.
When the world was over run with tyranny
The least remove therefrom was a glorious rescue.
But that it is imperfect, subject to convulsions, and
incapable
Of producing what it seems to promise, is easily
demonstrated.

Here, Paine urges a three-fifths vote on legislation in Congress, a permanent filibuster if you will, to guarantee all laws are a product of general, though not unanimous, agreement.

CS-120

I cannot help being sometimes surprised at the
complimentary references
Which I have seen and heard made to ancient histories
and transactions.
The wisdom, civil governments, and sense of honour
Of the states of Greece and Rome, are frequently
Held up as objects of excellence and imitation.
Mankind have lived to very little purpose,

Example from prior governments should not be overestimated. Most governments, ancient or modern, were or are tyrannies. It is to the few republics that America should be compared.

If, at this period of the world, they must
Go two or three thousand years back for lessons and examples.
We do great injustice to ourselves by placing them
In such a superior line. We have no just authority for it,
Neither can we tell why it is that we should suppose ourselves inferior.
Could the mist of antiquity be cleared away, and men
And things be viewed as they really were,
It is more than probable that they would admire us,
Rather than we them. America has surmounted
A greater variety and combination of difficulties,
Than, I believe, ever fell to the share of any one people,
In the same space of time, and has replenished the world
With more useful knowledge and sounder maxims of civil government
Than were ever produced in any age before.
Had it not been for America, there had been no such thing
As freedom left throughout the whole universe.
England has lost hers in a long chain of right reasoning
From wrong principles, and it is from this country, now,
That she must learn the resolution to redress herself,
And the wisdom how to accomplish it.
The Grecians and Romans were strongly possessed
Of the spirit of liberty but not the principle,
For at the time that they were determined not to be slaves themselves,
They employed their power to enslave the rest of mankind.
But this distinguished era is blotted by no one misanthropical vice.
In short, if the principle on which the cause is founded,
The universal blessings that are to arise from it,
The difficulties that accompanied it, the wisdom with which

Paine understood that the purpose of any constitution was both to define the government and to restrain it. He understood this far better after he was condemned to death by Robespierre in France and narrowly escaped the guillotine during The Terror in Paris.

It has been debated, the fortitude by which it has been supported,
The strength of the power which we had to oppose,
And the condition in which we undertook it,
Be all taken in one view, we may justly style it
The most virtuous and illustrious revolution
That ever graced the history of mankind.
A good opinion of ourselves is exceedingly necessary
In private life, but absolutely necessary in public life,
And of the utmost importance in supporting national character.
I have no notion of yielding the palm of the United States
To any Grecians or Romans that were ever born.
We have equaled the bravest in times of danger,
And excelled the wisest in construction of civil governments.
From this agreeable eminence let us take a review of present affairs.
The spirit of corruption is so inseparably interwoven
With British politics, that their ministry suppose
All mankind are governed by the same motives.
They have no idea of a people submitting even to
Temporary inconvenience from an attachment to rights and privileges.
Their plans of business are calculated by the hour and for the hour,
And are uniform in nothing but the corruption which gives them birth.
They never had, neither have they at this time,
Any regular plan for the conquest of America by arms.
They know not how to go about it,
Neither have they power to effect it if they did know.

AC-V-168

This last indignity gave a new spring to independence.
Those who knew the savage obstinacy of the king,
And the jobbing, gambling spirit of the court,
Predicted the fate of the petition, as soon as it was sent from America;
For the men being known, their measures were easily foreseen.
As politicians we ought not so much to ground our hopes
On the reasonableness of the thing we ask,
As on the reasonableness of the person of whom we ask it:
Who would expect discretion from a fool, candor
From a tyrant, or justice from a villain?
AC-III-131

Purple prose has its place in politics. When the cause is valid and circumstances dire, one should pull out all the stops in the use of invective. Quality outrage and invective died with H. L. Mencken.

The principal causes why independence has not
Been so universally supported as it ought,
Are fear and indolence, and the causes why it has been opposed,
Are, avarice, down-right villainy, and lust of personal power.
There is not such a being in America as a Tory from conscience;
Some secret defect or other is interwoven in the character of all those,
Be they men or women, who can look with patience
On the brutality, luxury and debauchery
Of the British court, and the violations of their army here.
A woman's virtue must sit very lightly
On her who can even hint a favorable sentiment in their behalf.
It is remarkable that the whole race of prostitutes
In New York were Tories; and the schemes
For supporting the Tory cause in this city,
For which several are now in jail, and one hanged,

Were concerted and carried on in common bawdy-houses,
Assisted by those who kept them.

AC-III-133

Regular turnover among elected officials was a common theme of many of the Framers. I leave it to the readers to determine whether current American officials "swim in the common sea" or whether they are "an interest separate from the electors."

Some convenient tree will afford them a State-House,
Under the branches of which, the whole colony
May assemble to deliberate on public matters.
It is more than probable that their first laws will have
The title only of regulations, and be enforced
By no other penalty than public disesteem.
In this first parliament every man, by natural right,
Will have a seat. But as the colony increases,
The public concerns will increase likewise,
And the distance at which the members may be separated,
Will render it too inconvenient for all of them to meet
On every occasion as at first, when their number was small,
Their habitations near, and the public concerns few and trifling.
This will point out the convenience of their consenting
To leave the legislative part to be managed by a select number
Chosen from the whole body, who are supposed to have
The same concerns at stake which those have
Who appointed them, and who will act in the same manner
As the whole body would act were they present.
If the colony continues increasing, it will become necessary
To augment the number of the representatives, and that
The interest of every part of the colony may be attended to,
It will be found best to divide the whole
Into convenient parts, each part sending its proper number;
And that the elected might never form to themselves
An interest separate from the electors, prudence will point out
The propriety of having elections often; because as the elected

Might by that means return and mix again
With the general body of the *electors* in a few months,
Their fidelity to the public will be secured by the prudent reflection
Of not making a rod for themselves.
And as this frequent interchange will establish
A common interest with every part of the community,
They will mutually and naturally support each other,
And on this (not on the unmeaning name of king)
Depends the *strength of government, and the happiness of the governed.*

CS-119

Telling the people what they want to hear—regardless of the truth—in order to get elected is nothing new.

. . . There is a dangerous species of popularity, which, I fear,
Some men are seeking from their constituents . . . ,
That if they are elected they will lighten their taxes; . . .
Which . . . cannot be done without exposing the country to . . . the enemy. . . .
Where knowledge is a duty ignorance is a crime;
And if any man whose duty it was to know better
Has encouraged such . . . , he has either deceived himself or them.

PG-285

Paine comments here on the Pennsylvania legislature, but might as well be writing about Congress. Washington and Madison would later rail against the evils of "faction" in government, which meant political parties. On this point,

When the majority of a single house is made upon
The ground of party prejudice, or fitted to be the dupes thereof,
That its government, instead of comprehending the good of the whole
Dispassionately and impartially, will be that of party favor and oppression. . . .
It was absolutely necessary that the prejudices of party
Should have no operation within the walls of the legislature;

For when it descends to this, a single legislature,
On account of the superabundance of its power,
And the uncontrolled rapidity of its execution, becomes
As dangerous to the principles of liberty as . . . a despotic
monarchy.
The present form was well intended,
But the abuse of its power operates to its destruction.
It withstood the opposition of its enemies,
And will fall through the misconduct of its friends.

all the Framers missed the mark. Parties cannot be eliminated; they can only be controlled.

At the commencement of the revolution, it was supposed
That . . . the executive part of the government was the
only dangerous part;
But we now see that quite as much mischief, if not more,
May be done, and as much arbitrary conduct acted, by a
legislature.

APA-360

After attacking the efforts of some legislators to separate the interests of farmers and merchants and pit them against each other as opponents, not partners, Paine concludes:

So long as it shall be the choice of the people to continue
The legislature in a single house, the circumstances of the
country
And the importance of the trust (being greater than that
Committed to any single body of men in any state in the
union)
Evidently require, that the men to be elected thereto
Be men freed from the bigotry and shackles of party,
Of liberal minds, and conversant in the means of
increasing
The riches of the state, and cultivating and extending the
prosperity thereof.

APA-362

Of course *it would be best that all members of any legislature be high-minded people, free of passion and party prejudices, but that is impossible. It is this truth that made the separation of powers between the branches of the federal government, and between the federal and state governments, absolutely essential to the survival of the Republic.*

Paine is referring to the members of Parliament who were elected from the "corporate towns," which were controlled by special interests. Unless the would-be member satisfied those interests, he would not be allowed to stand for one of these "safe" seats. Paine's use of the word "corporations" included districts controlled by guilds of specialized workers. Guilds were the precursors of today's unions. Readers can assess for themselves the degree to which American leaders today represent corporate interests.

As one of the Houses of the English Parliament is, in a great measure,
Made up of elections from these corporations;
And as it is unnatural that a pure stream should flow from a foul fountain,
Its vices are but a continuation of the vices of its origin.
A man of moral honour and good political principles
Cannot submit to the mean drudgery and disgraceful arts
By which such elections are carried.
To be a successful candidate, he must be destitute
Of the qualities that constitute a just legislator;
And being thus disciplined to corruption by the mode
Of entering into Parliament, it is not to be expected
That the representative should be better than the man.
RM-II-V-609

In casting our eyes over the world,
It is extremely easy to distinguish the governments which have
Arisen out of society, or out of the social compact,
From those which have not; . . . it will be proper
To take a review of the several sources from which governments
Have arisen and on which they have been founded.

They may be all comprehended under three heads.
First, Superstition. Secondly, Power. Thirdly,
The common interest of society and the common rights of man.
The first was a government of priestcraft, the second
Of conquerors, and the third of reason.
When a set of artful men pretended, through
The medium of oracles, to hold intercourse with the Deity,

As familiarly as they now march up the back-stairs in
European courts,
The world was completely under the government of
superstition.
The oracles were consulted, and whatever they were made
to say
Became the law; and this sort of government
Lasted as long as this sort of superstition lasted.
After these a race of conquerors arose, whose government,
Like that of William the Conqueror, was founded in power,
And the sword assumed the name of a scepter.
Governments thus established last as long
As the power to support them lasts; but that they might
Avail themselves of every engine in their favor,
They united fraud to force, and set up an idol
Which they called Divine Right, and which, in imitation
Of the Pope, who affects to be spiritual and temporal,
And in contradiction to the Founder of the Christian
religion,
Twisted itself afterwards into an idol of another shape, called
Church and State. The key of St. Peter
And the key of the Treasury became quartered on one
another,
And the wondering cheated multitude worshipped the
invention.
When I contemplate the natural dignity of man,
When I feel (for Nature has not been kind enough to me
To blunt my feelings) for the honour and happiness of its
character,
I become irritated at the attempt to govern mankind by
force and fraud,
As if they were all knaves and fools, and can scarcely
Avoid disgust at those who are thus imposed upon.

RM-I-466

Contrary to popular belief, the consulting of oracles has not disappeared in modern America. At the height of their powers, the Roman augurs were nine in number, wore special robes, and their decisions could not easily be questioned by anyone. In some decisions, the Supreme Court bends the Constitution to suit its own will. Other than that the augurs read chicken entrails and the justices read their own souls, what difference is there?

Paine offers these reasons why the legislature of any republic should not be composed of aristocracy in that republic. Do his arguments also apply to an aristocracy which installs itself and then exists for one generation, maybe two, as career politicians are capable of doing?

. . . There is an . . . unfitness in an aristocracy to be legislators for a nation.
Their ideas of distributive justice are corrupted at the very source.
They begin life by trampling on all their younger brothers and sisters,
And relations of every kind, and are taught and educated so to do.
With what ideas of justice or honour can that man enter a house of legislation,
Who absorbs in his own person
The inheritance of a whole family of children
Or doles out to them some pitiful portion with the insolence of a gift?
. . . The idea of hereditary legislators is as inconsistent as that of
Hereditary judges, or hereditary juries;
And as absurd as an hereditary mathematician,
Or an hereditary wise man; and as ridiculous as an hereditary poet laureate.
. . . A body of men, holding themselves accountable to nobody,
Ought not to be trusted by anybody.
. . . It is continuing the uncivilized principle of governments
Founded in conquest, and the base idea of man
Having property in man, and governing him by personal right.

RM-I-479

Every history of the creation, and every traditionary account,
Whether from the lettered or unlettered world, however they
May vary in their opinion or belief of certain particulars,
All agree in establishing one point,

The unity of man; by which I mean
That men are all of one degree,
And consequently that all men are born equal,
And with equal natural right, in the same manner
As if posterity had been continued by creation instead of generation,
The latter being the only mode by which the former is carried forward;
And consequently every child born into the world
Must be considered as deriving its existence from God.
The world is as new to him as it was to the first man that existed,
And his natural right in it is of the same kind.

RM-I-463

Natural rights are in disrepute in American law schools. The problem is not that they are hard to define; actually that is quite easy. Instead, the problem is that they are based on concepts common to the world's religions. Hostility to religion, not to rights, drives this bias.

The meaning, then, good people, of all this, is:
That government is governed by no principle whatever;
That it can make evil good, or good evil, just as it pleases.
In short, that government is arbitrary power.

RM-I-512

To see how well Paine's descriptions of ancient monarchies describe modern dictatorships equally well, compare Paine to Orwell's Animal Farm *and* Nineteen Eighty-Four.

Great part of that order which reigns among mankind
Is not the effect of government. It has its origin
In the principles of society and the natural constitution of man.
It existed prior to government, and would exist
If the formality of government was abolished.
The mutual dependence and reciprocal interest
Which man has upon man, and all the parts
Of civilized community upon each other,
Create that great chain of connection which holds it together.
The landholder, the farmer, the manufacturer,
The merchant, the tradesman, and every occupation,
Prospers by the aid which each receives from the other,

A subheading from Mark Twain neatly summarizes this political and economic analysis of Paine: "Let me make the superstitions of a nation and I care not who makes its law." The influence of Adam Smith's Wealth of Nations *is apparent in Paine's economic analysis. By happy coincidence, Smith's work was published in 1776. His theory of "the invisible hand"—which causes men, acting in their own self-interest, nonetheless to benefit each other and society—is receiving renewed interest today as the failures of "command economies" continue to rise and the alternative "market economies" continue to succeed. Singapore, not the Sudan, is the shape of the future. The recent economic collapses, both worldwide and domestic, do not change this analysis. The failures are still*

And from the whole. Common interest
Regulates their concerns, and forms their law;
And the laws which common usage ordains,
Have a greater influence than the laws of government.
In fine, society performs for itself almost everything
Which is ascribed to government.
To understand the nature and quantity of government proper
For man, it is necessary to attend to his character.
As Nature created him for social life,
She fitted him for the station she intended.
In all cases she made his natural wants greater than his individual powers.
No one man is capable, without the aid of society,
Of supplying his own wants, and those wants,
Acting upon every individual, impel the whole of them
Into society, as naturally as gravitation acts to a centre.
But she has gone further. She has
Not only forced man into society by a diversity of wants
Which the reciprocal aid of each other can supply,
But she has implanted in him a system of social affections,
Which, though not necessary to his existence,
Are essential to his happiness.
There is no period in life
When this love for society ceases to act.
It begins and ends with our being.
If we examine with attention
Into the composition and constitution of man,
The diversity of his wants, and the diversity of talents
In different men for . . . accommodating the wants of each other,
His propensity to society, and consequently to preserve
The advantages resulting from it, we shall easily discover,
That a great part of what is called government is mere imposition.

Government is no farther necessary than to supply the few
cases
To which society and civilization are not conveniently
competent;
And instances are not wanting to show, that everything
Which government can usefully add thereto, has been
Performed by the common consent of society, without
government.
For upwards of two years from the commencement of the
American War,
And to a longer period in several of the American States,
There were no established forms of government.
The old governments had been abolished,
And the country was too much occupied in defense
To employ its attention in establishing new governments;
Yet during this interval order and harmony were
preserved
As inviolate as in any country in Europe.
There is a natural aptness in man, and more so in society,
Because it embraces a greater variety of abilities and
resource,
To accommodate itself to whatever situation it is in.
The instant formal government is abolished,
Society begins to act: a general association takes place,
And common interest produces common security.
So far is it from being true, as has been pretended,
That the abolition of any formal government
Is the dissolution of society,
That it acts by a contrary impulse,
And brings the latter the closer together.
All that part of its organization which it had committed
To its government, devolves again upon itself,
And acts through its medium. When men,
As well from natural instinct as from reciprocal benefits,

greater in the command economies, which Smith and Paine both foresaw.

Free individuals acting together in free associations were, and by a slight margin still are, the heart of both America's economy and society.

Have habituated themselves to social and civilized life,
There is always enough of its principles in practice
To carry them through any changes they may find necessary
Or convenient to make in their government.
In short, man is so naturally a creature of society
That it is almost impossible to put him out of it.
Formal government makes but a small part of civilized life;
And when even the best that human wisdom can devise is established,
It is a thing more in name and idea than in fact.
It is to the great and fundamental principles of society
And civilization—to the common usage universally consented to,
And mutually and reciprocally maintained—
To the unceasing circulation of interest, which,
Passing through its million channels, invigorates
The whole mass of civilized man—it is to these things,
Infinitely more than to anything which even
The best instituted government can perform,
That the safety and prosperity of the individual and of the whole depends.
The more perfect civilization is, the less occasion has it
For government, because the more does it regulate its own affairs,
And govern itself; but so contrary is the practice of old governments
To the reason of the case, that the expenses of them
Increase in the proportion they ought to diminish.
It is but few general laws that civilized life requires,
And those of such common usefulness, that
Whether they are enforced by the forms of government or not,
The effect will be nearly the same.

If we consider what the principles are that first
Condense men into society, and what are the motives
That regulate their mutual intercourse afterwards,
We shall find, by the time we arrive at what is called
 government,
That nearly the whole of the business is performed
By the natural operation of the parts upon each other.
Man, with respect to all those matters,
Is more a creature of consistency than he is aware,
Or than governments would wish him to believe.
All the great laws of society are laws of nature.
Those of trade and commerce, whether with respect
To the intercourse of individuals or of nations,
Are laws of mutual and reciprocal interest.
They are followed and obeyed, because it is the interest
Of the parties so to do, and not on account
Of any formal laws their governments may impose or
 interpose.
But how often is the natural propensity to society
Disturbed or destroyed by the operations of government!
When the latter, instead of being ingrafted on the principles
Of the former, assumes to exist for itself, and acts
By partialities of favour and oppression, it becomes
The cause of the mischiefs it ought to prevent.

RM-II-I-551

Here, as in many other places in Paine's works, he shows that he believes in free markets to promote maximum prosperity for Americans. Those who do not understand the role of prices in a free market to promote economic efficiency and success should review Thomas Sowell's Basic Economics.

A constitution is the property of a nation, and not
Of those who exercise the government.
All the constitutions of America are declared to be
Established on the authority of the people.
In France, the word nation is used instead of the people;
But in both cases, a constitution is a thing antecedent
To the government, and always distinct there from.

RM-II-IV-578

The Constitution is the one possession all Americans have in common, our secular religion as Franklin observed. Presidents, congresses, justices come and go. But while in power, all tend to encroach on the Constitution by claiming powers they have no right to, and in doing that, diminishing our rights. In the short run, many objects claim more attention. In the long run, none is more important than preserving the Constitution as the will of the people.

It is self-evident that no constitution is perfect when established, nor could remain so if it were. Some method of amendment needs be provided. However, the right to make changes belongs to the people, in line with their will. In America, that means Congress by two-thirds vote and the state legislatures by three-fourths vote. The need for change is not a blank check to be cashed by the president, Congress, or the Supreme Court whenever they, *but not yet* the people, *think change is needed.*

The constitutions of America, and also that of France,
Have either affixed a period for their revision,
Or laid down the mode by which improvement shall be made. . . .
The Rights of Man are the rights of all generations of men,
And cannot be monopolized by any. . . .
The best constitution that could now be devised,
Consistent with the condition of the present moment,
May be far short of that excellence which a few years may afford.
There is a morning of reason rising upon man on
The subject of government, that has not appeared before.
RM-II-IV-594

Paine was almost never dead wrong in political analysis, but he was in this instance. He did not see the need of judges independent of both the president and Congress. He also argued for a unicameral legislature (as did Franklin)

Though all the constitutions of America are on one general principle,
Yet no two of them are exactly alike in their component parts,
Or in the distribution of the powers which they give
To the actual governments.
Some are more, and others less complex.
In forming a constitution, it is first necessary to consider
What are the ends for which government is necessary?
Secondly, what are the best means, and
The least expensive, for accomplishing those ends?
Government is nothing more than a national association;
And the object of this association is the good of all,
As well individually as collectively. Every man
Wishes to pursue his occupation, and to enjoy the fruits
Of his labours and the produce of his property in peace
And safety, and with the least possible expense.
When these things are accomplished, all the objects
For which government ought to be established are answered.
It has been customary to consider government

Under three distinct general heads.
The legislative, the executive, and the judicial.
But if we permit our judgment to act unencumbered
By the habit of multiplied terms, we can perceive
No more than two divisions of power, of which civil
government
Is composed, namely, that of legislating or enacting laws,
And that of executing or administering them.
Everything, therefore, appertaining to civil government,
Classes itself under one or other of these two divisions.
RM-II-IV-585

which might be better in theory, but ignores the reality of the Great Compromise, necessary to have any constitution at all coming out of the Philadelphia Convention.

Thus the several states have sent representatives to assemble
Together in Congress, and they have empowered that body,
Which thus becomes their center,
And are no other than themselves in representation,
To conduct and manage the war, while their constituents
At home attend to the domestic cares of the country,
Their internal legislation, their farms, professions
Or employments: For it is only by reducing
Complicated things to method and orderly connection
That they can be understood with advantage,
Or pursued with success. . . . For with respect to those
things
Which immediately concern the union,
And for which the union was purposely established,
And is intended to secure, each state
Is to the United States what each individual
Is to the state he lives in. And it is on this grand point,
This movement upon one centre,
That our existence as a nation, our happiness as a people,
And our safety as individuals, depend.
It may happen that some state or other may be
Somewhat over or under rated, but this cannot be much.

This anticipates and answers the Nullification Doctrine advanced by John Calhoun and the basis of the Southern secession. The nation cannot survive if individual states can pick and choose the federal laws they will obey. But the other side of that coin is this: the federal government should not claim for itself powers that rightfully belong to the states and citizens. That is exactly what the now-neglected Tenth Amendment provides for.

The experience which has been had upon the matter,
Has nearly ascertained their several abilities.
But even in this case, it can only admit of an appeal
To the United States, but cannot authorize any state
To make the alteration itself, any more than our internal government
Can admit an individual to do so in the case of an act of assembly;
For if one state can do it, then may another do the same,
And the instant this is done the whole is undone.
CSFW-304

The United States did defraud its soldiers of their pay in the Revolution, with great consequences. Daniel Shays, an unpaid veteran, lost his farm for want of £12 in unpaid debt and launched "Shays' Rebellion." That event helped cause the Constitutional Convention at which the failed Articles of Confederation were abandoned and a new and better government was created under the Constitution of the United States. One of the first acts of the new government was to guarantee the unpaid debts of the old one, including to the veterans who had served with honor but without pay.

Now if the sum which shall be raised should fall short,
Either by the several acts of the states for raising it,
Or by the manner of collecting it, the deficiency
Will fall on the fifth head, the soldiers' pay,
Which would be defrauding them, and eternally
Disgracing ourselves. It would be a blot on the councils,
The country, and the revolution of America,
And a man would hereafter be ashamed
To own that he had any hand in it. . . .
Now, I ask, why was all this done,
But from that extremely weak and expensive doctrine,
That the country could not bear it?
That is, that she could not bear, in the first instance,
That which would have saved her twice as much at last;
Or, in proverbial language, that she could not
Bear to pay a penny to save a pound;
The consequence of which . . . that she has paid a pound for a penny.
Why are there so many unpaid certificates
In almost every man's hands,
But from the parsimony of not providing sufficient revenues?
Besides, the doctrine contradicts itself; because,

If the whole country cannot bear it,
How is it possible that a part should?
And yet this has been the case: for those
Things have been had; and they must be had;
But the misfortune is, that they have been obtained
In a very unequal manner, and upon expensive credit,
Whereas, with ready money, they might have been
Purchased for half the price, and nobody distressed.

CSFW-301

In the resolution of Congress already recited, it is
recommended
To the several states *to lay taxes for raising their quotas*
Of money for the United States, separate from those
Laid for their own particular use.
This is a most necessary point to be observed,
And the distinction should follow all the way through.
They should be levied, paid and collected, separately,
And kept separate in every instance. Neither have
The civil officers of any state, nor the government of
that state,
The least right to touch that money which the people
Pay for the support of their army and the war,
Any more than Congress has to touch that
Which each state raises for its own use.

CSFW-306

It was the failure of tax policy above all else that caused the Articles of Confederation to fail. The central government could only beg money from the states. It had no adequate means to support itself.

Whatever commotions are produced in Republican states,
Are not produced by a Republican spirit, but by those
Who seek to extinguish it. A Republican state
Cannot produce its own destruction, it can only suffer it. . . .
All men are Republicans by nature and Royalists only by
fashion.

FL-III-80

Paine here presages what Benjamin Franklin said at the conclusion of the Constitutional Convention. With all our doctrinal disagreements, Americans have but one thing in common, the secular religion which is the Constitution of the United States. As it describes itself, it is the "supreme Law," and through its amendment powers it belongs to the people themselves but not to the government itself.

Yet that we may not appear to be defective even in earthly honours,
Let a day be solemnly set apart for proclaiming the charter;
Let it be brought forth placed on the divine law,
The word of God; let a crown be placed thereon,
By which the world may know,
That so far as we approve as monarchy,
That in America the Law is King.
For as in absolute governments the King is law,
So in free countries the law *ought* to be King;
And there ought to be no other. But lest any ill use
Should afterwards arise, let the crown at the conclusion of the ceremony
Be demolished, and scattered among the people whose right it is.

CS-152

"When we are planning for posterity,
We ought to remember,
That virtue is not hereditary."

Canto IV: On Leadership

IMMEDIATE necessity makes many things convenient,
Which if continued would grow into oppressions.
Expedience and right are different things.
When the calamities of America required a consultation,
There was no method so ready, or at that time so proper,
As to appoint persons from the several Houses of Assembly. . . .
And the wisdom with which they have proceeded
Hath preserved this continent from ruin.
But as it is more than probable that
We shall never be without a Congress,
Every well wisher to good order, must own,
That the mode for choosing members of that body, deserves consideration.
And I put it as a question to those, who make a study of mankind,
Whether representation and election is not too great a power
For one and the same body of men to possess?
When we are planning for posterity, we ought to remember,
That virtue is not hereditary.

CS-165

This is a very simple proposition, that those who currently hold power should not control the election of their replacements. Yet, isn't that the very purpose of seniority rules and gerrymandered districts?

A bad cause will ever be supported by bad means and bad men;
And whoever will be at the pains of examining strictly into things,

Though these words were written in a time of war, they apply equally to the practice of politics at any time. There have always been, and will always be, some men who will do anything, say anything, to carry the day with their chosen issues. Such men sully the name of leadership in any nation, in any time, in any cause.

Will find that one and the same spirit of oppression and impiety,
More or less, governs through your whole party in both countries:
Not many days ago, I accidentally fell in company
With a person of this city noted for espousing your cause,
And on my remarking to him, "that it appeared clear to me,
By the late providential turn of affairs,
That God Almighty was visibly on our side,"
He replied, "We care nothing for that
You may have Him, and welcome;
If we have but enough of the devil on our side, we shall do."
However carelessly this might be spoken, matters not,
'Tis still the insensible principle that directs all your conduct
And will at last most assuredly deceive and ruin you.
AC-II-107

All crises in American history have revealed some "disguised Tories" who oppose America's course not as a matter of principle, but because they neither understand nor respect this nation. Some citizen opponents act from principle; perhaps more act from disreputable motives.

Yet panics, in some cases, have their uses;
They produce as much good as hurt.
Their duration is always short; the mind soon
Grows through them, and acquires a firmer habit than before.
But their peculiar advantage is, that they are
The touchstones of sincerity and hypocrisy,
And bring things and men to light,
Which might otherwise have lain forever undiscovered.
In fact, they have the same effect on secret traitors,
Which an imaginary apparition would have upon a private murderer.
They sift out the hidden thoughts of man,
And hold them up in public to the world.
Many a disguised Tory has lately shown his head,
That shall penitentially solemnize with curses
The day on which Howe arrived upon the Delaware.
AC-I-92

Voltaire has remarked that King William never appeared
To full advantage but in difficulties and in action;
The same remark may be made on General Washington,
For the character fits him. There is a natural firmness
In some minds which cannot be unlocked by trifles,
But which, when unlocked, discovers a cabinet of fortitude;
And I reckon it among those kind of public blessings,
Which we do not immediately see, that God hath
Blessed him with uninterrupted health, and
Given him a mind that can even flourish upon care.

AC-I-94

If we inquire into the business of a king, we shall find
That in some countries they have none;
And after sauntering away their lives without pleasure to
themselves
Or advantage to the nation, withdraw from the scene,
And leave their successors to tread the same idle round.
In absolute monarchies the whole weight of business,
Civil and military, lies on the king;
The children of Israel in their request for a king,
Urged this plea "that he may judge us,
And go out before us and fight our battles."
But in countries where he is neither a judge nor a general,
As in England, a man would be puzzled to know what is
his business.

CS-134

The world now has some new constitutional monarchies. Among the most successful is Spain. The newest is Afghanistan. Wherever the monarch is only a symbol, and the actual government under him is a republic, none of the evils Paine described (other than the cost of his upkeep) still apply today.

The Speech if it may be called one,
Is nothing better than a wilful audacious libel
Against the truth, the common good, and the existence of
mankind;
And is a formal and pompous method of offering up
Human sacrifices to the pride of tyrants.

On the same day that Common Sense *was published in Philadelphia, there also appeared a speech by King George III arguing why America should submit to his benevolent rule and cease all talk of independence. History proved that Paine was a greater leader than George III—and it also proved again that "the pen is mightier than the sword" (Edward Bulwer-Lytton,* Richelieu, *II, ii).*

But this general massacre of mankind,
Is one of the privileges, and the certain consequence
Of Kings; . . . The Speech hath one good quality,
Which is, that it is not calculated to deceive,
Neither can we . . . be deceived by it.
Brutality and tyranny appear on the face of it.
It leaves us at no loss:
And every line convinces, even in the moment of reading,
That He, who hunts the woods for prey,
The naked and untutored Indian,
Is less a Savage than the King of Britain.
CS-Appendix-47

Power should never be hereditary, especially in a republic. The sons and daughters of powerful leaders should not be excluded from politics, but neither should they be automatically considered for the next available opening. Either they have the merits on their own to deserve public office, or they should be summarily rejected for lack of necessary wisdom or virtue—as any other unqualified candidate should be, regardless of who his parents were.

For all men being originally equals,
No one by birth could have a right to set up
His own family in perpetual preference to all others . . . ,
And though himself might deserve some decent degree
Of honours of his contemporaries, yet his descendants
Might be far too unworthy to inherit them.
One of the strongest natural proofs of the folly
Of hereditary right in kings, is, that nature disapproves it,
Otherwise, she would not so frequently turn it
Into ridicule by giving mankind an ass for a lion.
CS-130

Though I would carefully avoid giving unnecessary offence,
Yet I am inclined to believe, that all those
Who espouse the doctrine of reconciliation,
May be included within the following descriptions.
Interested men, who are not to be trusted;
Weak men, who cannot see;
Prejudiced men, who will not see;
And a certain set of moderate men, who
Think better of the European world than it deserves;

And this last class, by an ill-judged deliberation,
Will be the cause of more calamities to this continent,
Than all the other three.

CS-142

Sometimes those who seek change stay their hands because of too great a respect for the powers that be. A clear view of the power, virtue, and legitimacy of current leaders must be had before any contest against them.

To know whether it be the interest of the continent to be independent,
We need only ask this easy, simple question:
Is it the interest of a man to be a boy all his life?
The answer to one will be the answer to both.
America hath been . . . [a] scene of legislative contention
From the first king's representative to the last;
And this was unavoidably founded in the natural opposition
Of interest between the old country and the new.
A governor sent from England, or receiving his authority therefrom,
Ought never to have been considered in any other light
Than that of a genteel commissioned spy,
Whose private business was information, and his public business
A kind of civilized oppression. In the first of these characters
He was to watch the tempers, sentiments, and disposition of the people,
The growth of trade, and the increase of private fortunes;
And, in the latter, to suppress all such acts of the assemblies,
However beneficial to the people, which did not
Directly or indirectly throw some increase of power
Or profit into the hands of those that sent him.

AC-III-122

The first question about any leader is: for whom does he act? All leaders of any description couch their acts as being in "the interests of the people." The critical question about any leader is whether this claim is true or merely subterfuge. It is the nature of a republic that leaders are intended to act for the people because they answer to them in elections. This is the logic behind "no taxation without representation."

Men do not change from enemies to friends by the alteration of a name:
And in order to shew that reconciliation now is a dangerous doctrine,

In 1513 Niccolò Machiavelli wrote The Prince, *dedicated to Lorenzo the Magnificent. Among Machiavelli's advices were that the "appearance of virtue" is more important than the possession of virtue in a ruler. What Paine describes here was not new when he wrote it and remains applicable in governments today.*

I affirm, that it would be policy in the king at this time,
To repeal the acts for the sake of reinstating himself
In the government of the provinces; in order that he may
Accomplish by craft and subtility, in the long run,
What he cannot do by force and violence in the short one.
Reconciliation and ruin are nearly related.
CS-148

The usual honours of the dead . . . are not sufficiently sublime
To escort a character like you to the republic of dust and ashes;
For however men may differ in their ideas
Of grandeur or of government here,
The grave is nevertheless a perfect republic.
Death is not the monarch of the dead, but of the dying.
The moment he obtains a conquest he loses a subject,
And, like the foolish king you serve, will, in the end,
War himself out of all his dominions.
AC-V-152

As readers may gather, the following was addressed to King George III. It should be noted that saying or writing this statement was a hanging offense, as treason, had Paine ever been captured.

Never did a nation invite destruction upon itself
With the eagerness and the ignorance with which Britain has done.
Bent upon the ruin of a young and unoffending country,
She has drawn the sword that has wounded herself to the heart,
And in the agony of her resentment has applied a poison for a cure.
Her conduct towards America is a compound of rage and lunacy;

She aims at the government of it, yet preserves
Neither dignity nor character in her methods to obtain it.
Were government a mere manufacture or article of commerce,
Immaterial by whom it should be made or sold,
We might as well employ her as another,
But when we consider it as the fountain
From whence the general manners and morality
Of a country take their rise,
That the persons entrusted with the execution thereof are
By their serious example an authority to support these principles,
How abominably absurd is the idea of being hereafter governed
By a set of men who have been guilty of forgery, perjury,
Treachery, theft and every species of villainy
Which the lowest wretches on earth could practice or invent.
What greater public curse can befall any country
Than to be under such authority, and what greater blessing
Than to be delivered therefrom.
The soul of any man of sentiment would rise in brave rebellion
Against them, and spurn them from the earth.

AC-V-163

The character of any government is set by the character of its leaders. Paine here states a view shared by all the Framers that there is no separation between private and public virtue. This concept has largely disappeared in America today.

Painful as the task of speaking truth must sometimes be,
Yet I cannot avoid giving the following hint, because much,
Nay almost every thing depends upon it; and that is,
A *thorough knowledge of the persons whom we trust.*
It is the duty of the public, at this time, to scrutinize closely
Into the conduct of their Committee Members, Members of Assembly,
And Delegates to Congress; to know what they do, and their motives

"Committee Members" refers to those serving on the local Committees of Correspondence; the second, to the members of the state legislatures. This means local, state, and federal officials. It is the nature of the politician to ap-pear *to be a friend to every man and a supporter of (almost) every cause. Paine's advice that the public needs to know not only* what *they do, but* why *they do it remains as important as when he wrote these words.*

For so doing. Without knowing this, we shall
Never know who to confide in; but shall constantly
Mistake friends for enemies, and enemies for friends,
Till in the confusion of persons we sacrifice the cause.
FL-III-84

The tendency to use character assassination as a substitute for debate is not new in America. On the other hand, it may be more common today because the press and the public allow it to succeed. Creating "disaffection" has become a stock-in-trade of some special interest and political parties.

If every individual is to indulge his private malignancy,
Or his private ambition, and without any kind of proof,
All confidence will be undermined and all authority be destroyed.
Calumny is a species of treachery that ought to be punished
As well as any other kind of treachery.
It is a private vice, productive of a public evil,
Because it is possible to irritate men into disaffection
By continual calumny who never intended to be disaffected.
It is therefore, equally as necessary to guard against
The evils of unfounded or malignant suspicion
As against the evils of blind confidence.
It is equally as necessary to protect the characters of public
Officers from calumny as it is
To punish them for treachery or misconduct.
D-394

In the progress of politics, as in the common occurrences of life,
We are not only apt to forget
The ground we have traveled over,
But frequently neglect to gather up experience as we go.
We expend, if I may so say, the knowledge of every day
On the circumstances that produce it, and journey on
In search of new matter and new refinements:
But as it is pleasant and sometimes useful to look back,
Even to the first periods of infancy, and trace the turns
And windings through which we have passed,
So we may likewise derive many advantages

By halting a while in our political career,
And taking a review of the . . . labyrinth of little more
than yesterday.

Truly may we say, that never did men grow old in so short
a time!
We have crowded the business of an age
Into the compass of a few months, and have been
Driven through such a rapid succession of things,
That for the want of leisure to think, we unavoidably
Wasted knowledge as we came, and have left
Nearly as much behind us as we brought with us:
But the road is yet rich with the fragments, and, before we
Finally lose sight of them, will repay us
For the trouble of stopping to pick them up.
Were a man to be totally deprived of memory, he would
Be incapable of forming any just opinion;
Every thing about him would seem a chaos:
He would have even his own history to ask from every one;
And by not knowing how the world went in his absence,
He would be at a loss to know how it ought to go on
When he recovered, or rather, returned to it again.
In like manner, though in a less degree, a too great
Inattention to past occurrences retards
And bewilders our judgment in everything; while,
On the contrary, by comparing what is past with what is
present,
We frequently hit on the true character of both,
And become wise with very little trouble.
It is a kind of counter-march, by which
We get into the rear of time, and mark
The movements and meaning of things as we make our
return.
There are certain circumstances, which, at the time of
their happening,

Learning from history as it happens is an untidy process, but it is ultimately logical. People can learn too much, too little, or nothing at all from the same event. Understanding events is not possible unless one has a background of knowledge and the analytical skills to compare clearly the past and the present. Without naming names, the reporters who cover the White House and the Pentagon display a chronic lack of perspective and context. For them, every event is discrete, so they fail to see the sweep of history.

An understanding of cause and effect in public events is essential for public officials. Otherwise, they risk Einstein's definition of insanity, "doing the same thing over and over again and expecting different results."

Are a kind of riddle, and as every riddle
Is to be followed by its answer, so those kind
Of circumstances will be followed by their events,
And those events are always the true solution.
A considerable space of time may lapse between,
And unless we continue our observations from the one to the other,
The harmony of them will pass away unnoticed:
But the misfortune is, that partly from the pressing necessity
Of some instant things, and partly from
The impatience of our own tempers, we are . . .
In such a hurry to make out the meaning of everything
As fast as it happens, that we thereby never truly understand it;
And not only start new difficulties to ourselves by so doing,
But, as it were, embarrass Providence in her good designs.
I have been civil in stating this fault on a large scale,
For, as it now stands, it does not appear to be leveled
Against any particular set of men; but were it
To be refined a little further, it might . . . be applied
To the Tories with a degree of striking propriety:
Those men have been remarkable for drawing sudden conclusions
From single facts. The least apparent mishap on our side,
Or the least seeming advantage on the part of the enemy,
Have determined with them the fate of a whole campaign.
By this hasty judgment they have converted a retreat
Into a defeat; mistook generalship for error;
While every little advantage purposely given the enemy,
Either to weaken their strength by dividing it,
Embarrass their councils by multiplying their objects,
Or to secure a greater post by the surrender of a less,
Has been instantly magnified into a conquest.
Thus, by quartering ill policy upon ill principles,

They have frequently promoted the cause they designed to injure,
And injured that which they intended to promote.
AC-III-116

In another part of your proclamation [King George III] you say,
"But if the honours of a military life are become the object of the Americans,
Let them seek those honours under the banners of their rightful sovereign,
And in fighting the battles of the united British Empire,
Against our late mutual and natural enemies."
Surely! The union of absurdity with madness was never
Marked in more distinguishable lines than these.
Your rightful sovereign, as you call him, may do well enough for you,
Who dare not inquire into the humble capacities of the man;
But we, who estimate persons and things by their real worth,
Cannot suffer our judgments to be so imposed upon;
And unless it is your wish to see him exposed,
It ought to be your endeavor to keep him out of sight.
The less you have to say about him the better.
We have done with him, and that ought to be answer enough.
You have been often told so. Strange!
That the answer must be so often repeated.
You go a-begging with your king as with a brat,
Or with some unsaleable commodity you were tired of;
And though every body tells you no, no,
Still you keep hawking him about.
But there is one that will have him in a little time,
And as we have no inclination to disappoint you
Of a customer, we bid nothing for him. . . .
AC-VI-184

Sarcasm is a delicate tool in political debate. Those who cannot use it deftly are best advised to avoid it.

Paine addressed this comment to the British commissioners late in the war, when their cause was lost. It refers to them and to the remaining Tories who were clinging to their coattails for safety. I leave it to the reader to decide what groups of modern politicians would fit within these words.

But you are probably buoyed up by a set
Of wretched mortals, who, having deceived themselves,
Are cringing, with the duplicity of a spaniel,
For a little temporary bread.
Those men will tell you just what you please.
It is their interest to amuse, in order to lengthen out
Their protection. They study to keep you amongst them
For that very purpose; and in proportion as you
Disregard their advice, and grow callous to their complaints,
They will stretch into improbability,
And season their flattery the higher.
Characters like these are to be found in every country,
And every country will despise them.
AC-VI-189

Most elections serve only to choose those who will take office, but some serve a larger purpose. They smoke out those who oppose the people on an overriding issue—as in Pennsylvania in 1776, as in elections in times of crisis ever since then.

We have stood the experiment of the election,
For the sake of knowing the men who were against us.
Alas what are they? One half of them
Ought to be now asking public pardon
For their former offenses; and the other half may
Think themselves well off that they are let alone.
FL-IV-89

While Arnold commanded at West Point,
General Washington and the Minister of France went to
Hartford . . . , to consult on matters, in concert with
Admiral Terney,
Commander of the French fleet stationed at Rhode Island.
In the mean time Arnold held a conference with
Major Andre,
Adjutant-General to General Clinton, whom he
Traitorously furnished with plans of the fort,
State of the garrison, minutes of the last council of war,
And the manner in which he would post the troops

When the enemy should attempt a surprise;
And then gave him a pass, by the name of Mr. John
Anderson,
To go to the lines at the White Plains or lower,
If he Mr. Anderson thought proper, he being
(The pass said) on public business.
Thus furnished Andre parted from Arnold,
Set off for New York, and had nearly arrived
At the extent of our lines, when he was stopped
By a party of militia, to whom he produced his pass,
But they, not being satisfied with his account, insisted on
Taking him before the commanding officer, Lieut. Col.
Jamieson.
Finding himself in this situation, and hoping to escape by
a bribe,
He offered them his purse, watch and a promise
Of any quantity of goods they would accept,
Which these honest men nobly and virtuously scorned,
And confident with their duty took him to the proper
officer.
On examination there was found on him the above
mentioned papers
And several others, all in the handwriting of General
Arnold,
And finding himself thus detected, he confessed
His proper name and character. He was accordingly
Made a close prisoner, and the papers sent off by express
To West Point, at which place General Washington
Had arrived soon after the arrival of the packet. . . .
When we take a review of the history of former times
It will turn out to the honour of America that,
Notwithstanding the trying variety of her situation,
This is the only instance of defection in a general officer;
And even in this case, the unshaken honesty of those

This is the tale of betrayal by General Benedict Arnold. Then, as now, most betrayals of American interests are done for money, not for beliefs. There will always be those—a few in the military, a few political leaders, a few civilians—who will sell out the nation for financial gain. In a twist with a modern feel to it, Major André sought to bribe his way out of capture and exposure. How many modern malefactors have used bribery as a means to escape exposure and punishment? Major André was convicted by a military tribunal. Washington offered to exchange him for Arnold. General Clinton refused, so André was hanged.

Who detected him heightens the national character,
To which his apostasy serves as a foil.
From the nature of his crime, and his disposition to monopolize,
It is reasonable to conclude he had few or no direct accomplices.
His sole object was to make a monied bargain;
And to be consistent with himself, he would as readily betray
The side he has deserted to, as that he deserted from.
AC-CE-250

This is a classic description of failed public policy. It applies with equal accuracy to the British attempt to reduce America as it does to the last fifty years of policies concerning public education in America.

For everything which has been predicted has happened,
And all that was promised has failed.
A long series of politics so remarkably distinguished
By a succession of misfortunes, without one alleviating turn,
Must certainly have something in it systematically wrong.
It is sufficient to awaken the most credulous into suspicion,
And the most obstinate into thought. Either the means
In your power are insufficient, or the measures ill planned;
Either the execution has been bad,
Or the thing attempted impracticable; or, to speak more emphatically,
Either you are not able or heaven is not willing.
AC-VII-191

Often published with The American Crisis *is Paine's letter to Sir Guy Carleton. It consists entirely of a plea for the life of a British officer. Captain Huddy of the Jersey militia was captured and*

Though I can think no man innocent who has lent his hand
To destroy the country which he did not plant,
And to ruin those that he could not enslave,
Yet, abstracted from all ideas of right and wrong
On the original question, Captain Asgill,
In the present case, is not the guilty man.
The villain and the victim are here separated characters.
You hold the one and we the other.
You disown, or affect to disown and reprobate
The conduct of Lippencut, yet you give him a sanctuary;

And by so doing you as effectually become the executioner
Of Asgill, as if you had put the rope on his neck,
And dismissed him from the world.
Whatever your feelings on this interesting occasion may be
Are best known to yourself. Within the grave
Of your own mind lies buried the fate of Asgill.
He becomes the corpse of your will, or the survivor of
your justice.
Deliver up the one, and you save the other;
Withhold the one, and the other dies by your choice. . . .
But to protect him, be he who he may, is to patronize his
crime,
And to trifle it off by frivolous and unmeaning inquiries,
Is to promote it. There is no declaration you can make,
Nor promise you can give that will obtain credit.
It is the man and not the apology that is demanded. . . .
The evil must be put an end to; and the choice of persons
Rests with you. But if your attachment to the guilty is
stronger
Than to the innocent, you invent a crime that must destroy
Your character, and if the cause of your king needs to be
so supported,
For ever cease, sir, to torture our remembrance
With the wretched phrases of British honour,
British generosity and British clemency. . . .
They have been trained like hounds to the scent of blood,
And cherished in every species of dissolute barbarity.
Their ideas of right and wrong are worn away
In the constant habitude of repeated infamy,
Till, like men practiced in execution, they feel not
The value of another's life. The task before you,
Though painful, is not difficult; give up the murderer,
And save your officer, as the first outset of a necessary
reformation.

GC-335

taken to New York as a prisoner of war. Three weeks later, by order of a British officer named Lippencut, he was brought to the Jersey shore and hanged, with his body left hanging as a warning to the rebels. This action was contrary to the law of war and Washington demanded that General Clinton surrender his murdering officer. Instead, Clinton gave up Captain Asgill of the Guards, chosen by lot. So in the interests of justice, like John Adams, who carried the defense of the British soldiers after the Boston Massacre, Paine argued to spare the life of Asgill, set to be hanged for the offense of another.

That there are men in all countries who get their living by
war,
And by keeping up the quarrels of Nations, is as shocking
As it is true; but when those who are concerned
In the government of a country, make it
Their study to sow discord and cultivate prejudices
Between Nations, it becomes the more unpardonable.
RM-Preface-435

Time and again Paine returns to the theme that nations, like men, have characters determined by their deeds, for good or ill. Both men and nations depend on the credit of others, and when character is gone, credit falls with it.

The people of America have for years accustomed
themselves
To think and speak so freely and contemptuously of
English authority, and the inveteracy is so deeply rooted,
That a person invested with any authority from that
country,
And attempting to exercise it here, would have
The life of a toad under a harrow.
They would look on him as an interloper,
To whom their compassion permitted a residence. . . .
It would be a station of degradation,
Debased by our pity, and despised by our pride,
And would place England in a more contemptible
situation
Than any she has yet been in during the war.
We have too high an opinion of ourselves,
Even to think of yielding again the least obedience
To outlandish authority; and for a thousand reasons,
England would be the last country in the world
To yield it to. She has been treacherous,
And we know it. Her character is gone,
And we have seen the funeral. . . .
Must we not look upon you as a confederated body
Of faithless, treacherous men, whose assurances
Are fraud, and their language deceit?

What opinion can we possibly form of you,
But that you are a lost, abandoned, profligate nation,
Who sport even with your own character, and are
To be held by nothing but the bayonet or the halter?

AC-XII-344

Character is much easier kept than recovered,
And that man, if any such there be, who,
From sinister views, or littleness of soul,
Lends unseen his hand to injure it,
Contrives a wound it will never be in his power to heal.

AC-XIII-351

As George Washington observed in his farewell address, there is no permanent affection in international affairs. But there is respect based on conduct.

Yet let but a nation conceive rightly of its character,
And it will be chastely just in protecting it.
None ever began with a fairer than America and none
Can be under a greater obligation to preserve it.

AC-XIII-350

"...It is infinitely wiser and safer to form
A constitution of our own in a cool deliberate manner...
Than to trust such an interesting event to time and chance."

Canto V: On the Public Good

A GOVERNMENT of our own is our natural right: and when
A man seriously reflects on the precariousness of human affairs,
He will become convinced, that it is infinitely wiser and safer
To form a constitution of our own in a cool deliberate manner,
While we have it in our power, than to trust
Such an interesting event to time and chance.
If we omit it now, some Massenello may hereafter arise,
Who laying hold of popular disquietudes, may
Collect together the desperate and discontented,
And by assuming to themselves the powers of government,
May sweep away the liberties of the continent like a deluge.
[Massenello was a Naples fisherman, who in the space of a day led his city to throw off the rule of Spain, and make him the Neopolitan King.]

CS-153

In support of ratification of the new constitution eleven years later, Alexander Hamilton, in the Federalist No. 1, *wrote these words that echo both the hopes and fears expressed by Paine: "Happy will it be if our choice should be directed by a judicious estimate of our true interests, unperplexed and unbiased by considerations not connected with the public good. . . . The plan offered to our deliberations affects too many particular interests . . . not to involve in its discussion a variety of objects foreign to its merits, and of views, passions, and prejudices little favorable to the discovery of the truth."*

But as there is a peculiar delicacy, from whom,
Or in what manner, this business must first arise,
And as it seems most agreeable and consistent
That it should come from some intermediate body
Between the governed and the governors, that is,
Between the Congress and the people, let a

We tend to overlook in our quick histories that the United States has had two governments, not one. The first was the Articles of Confederation, which were already clearly failing when the final state, Maryland, ratified them. The Articles were written by Congress, not by a special body chosen for the sole purpose of drafting them. The Constitutional Convention, which did succeed, was conducted as Paine here suggests.

The right understanding of the Constitution of the United States can be drawn from this passage. Those who wrote it are long dead, except for the thousands of men and women who participated in 1992 in ratifying the Twenty-Seventh Amendment. Absent an amendment clause, the Constitution would be the dead hand of the past controlling the living. With that

Continental Conference be held,
In the following manner, and for the following purpose.

The conferring members being met, let their business be
To frame a Continental Charter,
Or Charter of the United Colonies;
(Answering to what is called the Magna Charta of England)
Fixing the number and manner of choosing members of Congress,
Members of Assembly, with their date of sitting,
And drawing the line of business and jurisdiction between them:
(Always remembering, that our strength is continental,
Not provincial:) Securing freedom and property
To all men, and above all things,
The free exercise of religion, according to the dictates
Of conscience; with such other matter as is necessary
For a charter to contain. Immediately after which,
The said Conference to dissolve, and the bodies
Which shall be chosen conformable to the said charter,
To be the legislators and governors of this continent for the time being:
Whose peace and happiness, may God preserve, Amen.
CS-151

It requires but a very small glance of thought
To perceive that although laws made in one generation
Often continue in force through succeeding generations,
Yet they . . . derive their force from the consent of the living.
A law not repealed continues in force,
Not because it *cannot* be repealed,
But because it *is not* repealed;
And the non-repealing passes for consent.
RM-I-441

A constitution is not a thing in name only,
But in fact. It has not an ideal, but a real existence;
And wherever it cannot be produced in a visible form,
There is none. A constitution is a thing antecedent
To a government, and a government is only the creature
Of a constitution. The constitution of a country
Is not the act of its government, but of the people
Constituting its government. It is the body of elements,
To which you can refer, and quote article by article;
And which contains the principles on which the government
Shall be established, the manner in which it shall be
organized,
The powers it shall have, the mode of elections, the duration
Of Parliaments, or by what other name such bodies may
be called;
The powers which the executive part of the government
shall have;
And in fine, everything that relates to the complete
organization
Of a civil government, and the principles on which it shall
act,
And by which it shall be bound. A constitution, therefore,
Is to a government what the laws made afterwards
By that government are to a court of judicature.
The court of judicature does not make the laws,
Neither can it alter them; it only acts
In conformity to the laws made and the government
Is in like manner governed by the constitution.

RM-I-467

clause, it stands firm with the consent of each new generation. The Constitution must be, and is, as it describes itself—the "supreme Law." It remains in effect until the people choose to change it.

This is a clearer and more accurate definition of a constitution—and the relationships it creates—than on a bad day, and in a bad case, can be mustered by a majority of the modern Supreme Court.

Should any body of men be hereafter delegated
For this or some similar purpose, I offer them
The following extracts from that wise observer on
governments

Dragonetti. "The science" says he "of the politician consists
In fixing the true point of happiness and freedom.
Those men would deserve the gratitude of ages,
Who should discover a mode of government
That contained the greatest sum of individual happiness,
With the least national expense."

"Dragonetti on virtue and rewards."
CS-152

The difference between the views of Paine and those of proponents of "civil disobedience" like Gandhi and Thoreau is not as great as it seems. The tactic of passive resistance was tried for two years in America before matters came to a head, shots were fired, and the Revolution began. Until war becomes the answer, civil behavior is the better choice.

I have always held it an opinion (making it always my practice)
That it is better to obey a bad law, making use
At the same time of every argument
To shew its errors and procure its repeal,
Than forcibly to violate it; because the precedent
Of breaking a bad law might weaken the force, and lead
To to a discretionary violation, of those which are good.
RM-II-Preface-545

The encouragement and protection of
The good subjects of any state,
And the suppression and punishment of bad ones,
Are the principal objects for which all authority is instituted,
And the line in which it ought to operate.
AC-III-142

Our . . . success depend[s] on such a variety of men and circumstances,
That every one who does but wish well,
Is of some use: there are men
Who have a strange awkwardness to arms,
Yet have hearts to risk every shilling in the cause,
Or in support of those who have better talents
For defending it. Nature, in the arrangement

Of mankind, has fitted some for every service in life:
Were all soldiers, all would starve and go naked,
And were none soldiers, all would be slaves.

AC-III-134

The people of Paris may say that they will not give
More than a certain price for provisions,
But as they cannot compel the country people to bring
Provisions to market the consequences will be directly contrary
To their expectations, and they will find
Dearness and famine instead of plenty and cheapness.
They may force the price down upon the stock in hand,
But after that the market will be empty.

D-393

Here's why price controls always fail in the long run. They are contrary to market reality; they are attempts to make water run uphill. Yet Congress and state legislatures still repeat the errors of the French Assembly in 1793. This error is particularly common among dictatorships. Because the "supreme leader" (by whatever name) knows that he can cow individuals to his will, and cause the legislature to pass whatever he chooses, he thinks he is immune to the laws of economics, and that, by decree, he can lower the price of bread.

Whoever has made the observation on the characters of nations
Will find it generally true, that the manners of a nation,
Or of a party, can better be ascertained the character
Of its press than from any other public circumstance.
If its press is licentious, its manners are not good.
Nobody believes a common liar, or a common defamer. . . .

Nothing is more common with printers, especially
Of newspapers, than the continual cry of *liberty of the press*,
As if because they are printers they are to have
More privileges than other people. . . .

Prior to what is called in England *the revolution*,
Which was in 1688, no work could be published
In that country without first obtaining the permission
Of an officer appointed by the government for inspecting works
Intended for publication. The same was the case

Paine demonstrates in these five paragraphs a better understanding of the meaning of a free press than most members of the modern press—or a majority of the Supreme Court—can currently muster.

In France, except that in France there were
Forty who were called *censors*, and in England
There was but one, called Imprematеur.

At the revolution the office of Imprematеur was abolished
And as works could then be published without
First obtaining the permission of the government officer,
The press was, in consequence of that abolition,
Said to be free, and it was from this circumstance
That the term *liberty of the press* arose. . . .

The term refers to the fact of printing *free*
From prior restraint, and not at all to the matter
Printed whether good or bad. The public
At large, or in the case of prosecution, a jury
Of the country will be the judges of the matter.
LP-429

Freedom of the press is an essential liberty not just for the press itself, but for the public. It does not mean, and should not mean, however, the "freedom" to publish anything, without consequences, just for the results. That is the direction in which lawyers with cases to win, and judges with agendas, have pushed the First Amendment recently. And Paine's comment about trial lawyers being "like Swiss soldiers" unfortunately remains true.

A man does not ask liberty before hand to say
Something he has a mind to say, but he becomes
Answerable afterwards for the atrocities he may utter.
In like manner, if a man makes the press utter
Atrocious things he becomes answerable for them
As if he had uttered them by word of mouth.
Mr. Jefferson has said in his inaugural speech, that,
"Error of opinion might be tolerated
When reason was left free to combat it."
This is sound philosophy in cases of error.
But there is a difference between error and licentiousness.

Some lawyers in defending their clients (for the generality
Of lawyers like Swiss soldiers will fight on either side)
Have often given their opinion of what they
Defined the liberty of the press to be. One said
It was this; another said it was that,

And so on, according to the case they were pleading.
LP-430

If I owe a person money, and cannot pay him,
And he threatens to put me in prison, another person
Can take the debt upon himself, and pay it for me;
But if I have committed a crime, every circumstance
Of the case is changed; moral Justice cannot take
The innocent for the guilty, even if the innocent would
Offer itself. To suppose Justice to do this,
Is to destroy the principle of its existence,
Which is the thing itself; it is then
No longer Justice, it is indiscriminate revenge.
AR-I-685

Paine makes this comment in a long discussion of why Virginia should relinquish its claim to 4,000 million acres out to the Pacific Ocean. Paine, of course, did not know of the Louisiana Purchase or of the Northwest Ordinance to fill that land with new states. Still, he understood America's destiny to be a continental power by creating, populating, and admitting new states.

Lands are the real riches of all the habitable world
And the natural funds of America. The funds of other
Countries are, in general, artificially constructed; . . .
Dependent upon credit, and always exposed to hazard . . . .
But lands can neither be annihilated nor lose their value;
On the contrary, they universally rise with population,
And rapidly so, when under the security of effective
government.
PG-283

The natural rights of man, and constitutional rights, are trivialized by a tide of claims that whatever anyone labels a "right" must be so and must be honored.

. . . There is a strange propensity in mankind to shelter
themselves under
The sanction of a right, however unreasonable that supposed right may be.
PG-278

They say Paper Money has improved the country—
Paper Money carried on the war,
And Paper Money did a great many other fine things.

When Paine wrote this, America's first government under the Articles of Confederation was collapsing. Our ambassadors were well-dressed beggars—borrowing money at upwards of 13 percent interest (including charges) from the Dutch—to meet current bills. This financial collapse led to the Constitutional Convention which in turn created the Constitution to replace the Articles.

Not one syllable of this is truth;
It is all error from beginning to end.
It was *credit* which did those things,
And that credit has failed, by non-performance,
And by the country being involved in debt and
The levity and instability of government measures. . . .

The fundamental principles of civil government are security
Of our rights and persons as freeman, and security of property.
A tender law, therefore, cannot stand on the principles
Of civil government, because it operates to take away
A man's share of civil and natural freedom,
And to render property insecure.
PM-364

If a man engages to sell and deliver a quantity of wheat,
He is not to deliver rye, any more than he who
Contracts to pay in hard money is at liberty
To pay in paper or in any thing else.
Those contracts . . . have expressed the legal tender on both sides,
And no . . . presumptuous authority of any assembly can . . . alter them.

This was a defect in both federal and state governments prior to the Constitution and explains why it prohibits both "ex post facto" and impairment of contract laws from Congress and from state legislatures.

This principle of civil government extends
To property as well as to life; . . .
Both of these cases must be referred to the laws existing
At the time the crime was done or the bargain made.
Each party then knew the relative situation
They stood in with each other, and on that law and that knowledge
They acted, and by no other can they be adjudged.
PM-366

Some writers have so confounded society with government,
As to leave little or no distinction between them;
Whereas they are not only different, but have different origins.
Society is produced by our wants, and government by wickedness;
The former promotes our happiness
Positively by uniting our affections,
The latter negatively by restraining our vices.
The one encourages intercourse, the other creates distinctions.
The first is a patron, the last a punisher.

CS-117

The tendency to confuse society with government is more pronounced in our day than in Paine's. Doing so either reduces the importance of society or inflates that of government. Either way, it is wrong.

. . . At the time when the taxes were very low, the poor were able
To maintain themselves; and there were no poor-rates.
In the present state of things a labouring man,
With a wife or two or three children, does not pay less
Than between seven and eight pounds a year in taxes.
He is not sensible of this, because it is disguised
To him in the articles which he buys, and he thinks
Only of their dearness; but as the taxes take from him,
At least, a fourth part of his yearly earnings,
He is consequently disabled from providing for a family,
Especially, if himself, or any of them, are afflicted with sickness. . . .
To pay as a remission of taxes to every poor family,
Out of the surplus taxes, and in room of poor-rates,
Four pounds a year for every child
Under fourteen years of age; enjoining the parents
Of such children to send them to school,
To learn reading, writing, and common arithmetic;
The ministers of every parish, of every denomination

The creation of social security to save the elderly from starvation is credited to Otto von Bismarck in Germany in 1889. However, Paine laid out a humane plan for the elderly and the poor a century earlier.

These are only highlights from Paine's analysis of groups within England who might need assistance, by numbers, cost, and impact on the British budget. Two things about this are remarkable. First, his plan encompasses aid for the poor, the elderly, public schools, and vocational education, all obvious subjects today, but extraordinary for a writer in the eighteenth century. The second remarkable fact is that he concluded that the British tax rates could be lowered *by these reforms. That tax rate was 25 percent, or about half of the total tax burden of local, state, and federal governments in America today. And Paine's main point was that the aid should go into the hands of those who needed it, rather than into organizations and staffs who would, as a profession, assist the needy—a surpris-*

To certify jointly to an office, for that purpose,
That this duty is performed.
The amount of this expense will be, For six hundred
And thirty thousand children at four pounds
Per annum each £2,520,000
By adopting this method, not only the poverty of the parents
Will be relieved, but ignorance will be banished
From the rising generation, and the number of poor
Will hereafter become less, because their abilities,
By the aid of education, will be greater.
Many a youth, with good natural genius,
Who is apprenticed to a mechanical trade, such as a carpenter,
Joiner, millwright, shipwright, blacksmith, etc.,
Is prevented getting forward the whole of his life
From the want of a little common education when a boy. . . .
To pay to every such person of the age
Of fifty years, and until he shall arrive
At the age of sixty, the sum of six pounds
Per annum out of the surplus taxes, and ten pounds
Per annum during life after the age of sixty. . . .
This support, as already remarked, is not of the nature
Of a charity but of a right. Every person in England,
Male and female, pays on an average in taxes
Two pounds eight shillings and sixpence per annum
From the day of his (or her) birth; and,
If the expense of collection be added,
He pays two pounds eleven shillings and sixpence; . . .
After all the above cases are provided for
There will still be a number of families who,
Though not properly of the class of poor,
Yet find it difficult to give education
To their children; and such children,
Under such a case, would be in a worse condition

Than if their parents were actually poor.
A nation under a well-regulated government should permit
None to remain uninstructed. It is monarchical and
aristocratical
Government only that requires ignorance for its support.
Suppose, then, four hundred thousand children
To be in this condition, . . . the method will be:
To allow for each of those children ten shillings
A year for the expense of schooling for six years each,
Which will give them six months schooling each year,
And half a crown a year for paper and spelling books. . . .
All the navies now in existence shall be put back,
Suppose to one-tenth of their present force.
This will save to France and England, at least
Two millions sterling annually to each,
And their relative force be in the same proportion as it is
now.
If men will permit themselves to think, as rational beings
Ought to think, nothing can appear
More ridiculous and absurd, exclusive of
All moral reflections, than to be
At the expense of building navies, filling them with men,
And then hauling them into the ocean,
To try which can sink each other fastest.
Peace, which costs nothing, is attended with
Infinitely more advantage, than any victory with all its
expense.
But this, though it best answers the purpose of nations,
Does not that of court governments, whose habited policy
Is pretense for taxation, places, and offices.

RM-II-V-625

But as we can securely defend and keep the country
For one third less than what our burden would be

ingly modern concept. In the last excerpt, Paine is discussing the "peace dividend," and he includes veteran's relief as well. Paine's conclusion was that competent government can obtain far better results for far less money if it applies reason to the forms of public welfare. Again, he was far ahead of his time, but he ignored one central fact: all government programs have "constituents," people with vested interests in seeing them continue, even if in truth the programs are flawed or total failures. Though his analysis is correct, applying it in the real world demands a level of courage that many politicians lack.

Paine knew how to appeal to practical concerns and not just use lofty statements of theory. He also knew how to use humor. His line about the miser as "idiot" recalls Mark Twain: "Suppose you were an idiot and suppose you were a member of Congress. But I repeat myself."

If it was conquered, and support the governments
Afterwards for one eighth of what Britain would levy on us,
And could I find a miser whose heart never felt the emotion
Of a spark of principle, even that man, uninfluenced
By every love but the love of money, and capable
Of no attachment but to his interest, would and must,
From the frugality which governs him, contribute to the defense
Of the country, or he ceases to be a miser and becomes an idiot.
But when we take in with it every thing that can ornament mankind;
When the line of our interest becomes the line of our happiness;
When all that can cheer and animate the heart,
When a sense of honour, fame, character, at home
And abroad, are interwoven not only with the security
But the increase of property, there exists not a man in America,
Unless he be an hired emissary, who does not see
That his good is connected with keeping up a sufficient defense.
AC-CE-241

I have already stated the number of souls in America
To be three millions, and by a calculation that I have made,
Which I have every reason to believe is sufficiently correct,
The whole expense of the war, and the support of the several governments,
May be defrayed for two million pounds sterling annually;
Which, on an average, is thirteen shillings and four pence
Per head, men, women, and children, and the peace establishment
At the end of the war will be but three quarters of a million,

Or five shillings sterling per head.
Now, throwing out of the question everything of honour,
Principle, happiness, freedom, and reputation in the world,
And taking it up on the simple ground of interest,
I put the following case:
Suppose Britain was to conquer America,
And, as a conqueror, was to lay her under no other conditions
Than to pay the same proportion towards her annual revenue
Which the people of England pay: our share, in that case,
Would be six million pounds sterling yearly.
Can it then be a question, whether it is best to raise two millions
To defend the country, and govern it ourselves,
And only three quarters of a million afterwards,
Or pay six millions to have it conquered,
And let the enemy govern it? Can it
Be supposed that conquerors would choose to put
Themselves in a worse condition than what
They granted to the conquered?
In England, the tax on rum is five shillings
And one penny sterling per gallon,
Which is one silver dollar and fourteen coppers.
Now would it not be laughable to imagine,
That after the expense they have been at,
They would let either Whig or Tory drink it cheaper than themselves?
Coffee, which is so inconsiderable an article of consumption
And support here, is there loaded with a duty
Which makes the price between five and six shillings per pound,
And a penalty of fifty pounds sterling on any person
Detected in roasting it in his own house.

Paine here talks about taxes that are "hidden" in the cost of goods. This is the very nature of the value added tax. Everything gets more expensive, but unlike sales tax, it does not appear on the receipt.

Readers can decide for themselves whether taxation in the United States today more resembles the British taxation which ended upon winning the war or the American taxation which was ours at the victory. Query what would happen if American products contained a "truth in taxation" label—stating with precision all the taxes that went into a product, as well as its ingredients.

There is scarcely a necessary of life that you can eat,
Drink, wear, or enjoy, that is not there loaded with a tax;
Even the light from heaven is only permitted
To shine into their dwellings by paying
Eighteen pence sterling per window annually;
And the humblest drink of life, small beer,
Cannot there be purchased without a tax of nearly
Two coppers per gallon, besides a heavy tax upon the malt,
And another on the hops before it is brewed, exclusive
Of a land-tax on the earth which produces them.
In short, the condition of that country, in point of taxation,
Is so oppressive, the number of her poor so great,
And the extravagance and rapaciousness of the court
So enormous, that, were they to effect a conquest of America,
It is then only that the distresses of America would begin.
Neither would it signify anything to a man
Whether he be Whig or Tory.
The people of England, and the ministry of that country,
Know us by no such distinctions.
What they want is clear, solid revenue,
And the modes which they would take to procure it,
Would operate alike on all.
Their manner of reasoning would be short,
Because they would naturally infer, that if we were able
To carry on a war of five or six years against them,
We are able to pay the same taxes which they do.
AC-CE-238

Britain did not go to war with America for the sake
Of dominion, because she was then in possession;
Neither was it for the extension of trade and commerce,
Because she had monopolized the whole,
And the country had yielded to it; neither was it

To extinguish what she might call rebellion,
Because before she began no resistance existed.
It could then be from no other motive than avarice,
Or a design of establishing, in the first instance,
The same taxes in America as are paid in England
(Which, as I shall presently show, are above eleven times
heavier
Than the taxes we now pay for the present year, 1780)
Or, in the second instance, to confiscate
The whole property of America, . . . and conquest
Of the latter, of which she had then no doubt.

AC-CE-235

Whatever other subjects arise, at heart all discussions about government are about taxation. "The power to tax involves the power to destroy." —Chief Justice John Marshall in McCulloch v. Maryland *(1819)*

Men whose political principles are founded on avarice,
Are beyond the reach of reason, and the only cure
Of Toryism of this cast is to tax it.
A substantial good drawn from a real evil,
Is of the same benefit to society, as if drawn from a virtue;
And where men have not public spirit
To render themselves serviceable,
It ought to be the study of government
To draw the best use possible from their vices.
When the governing passion of any man, or set of men,
Is once known, the method of managing them is easy;
For even misers, whom no public virtue can impress,
Would become generous, could a heavy tax be laid upon
covetousness.

AC-III-142

This is the basic philosophy of "sin" taxes on alcohol, tobacco, and the like. If a vice can't be prevented, it can at least be profitable to the government. The same principle applies to public lotteries.

Every passion that acts upon mankind
Has a peculiar mode of operation.
Many of them are temporary and fluctuating;
They admit of cessation and variety. But
Avarice is a fixed, uniform passion.

It neither abates of its vigor nor changes its object;
And the reason why it does not, is founded in the nature of things,
For wealth has not a rival where avarice is a ruling passion.
One beauty may excel another,
And extinguish from the mind of man
The pictured remembrance of a former one:
But wealth is the phoenix of avarice, and therefore
It cannot seek a new object,
Because there is not another in the world.
AC-CE-242

There is general agreement in America today that the Internal Revenue Code is a monster and that its collectors are often "burglars with badges." However, there is no agreement on what to use in place of the code. Sales tax and flat tax are the two main alternatives, and each of those share the virtues Paine describes—easy to collect and self-assessing by our own choices.

There are many reasons why a duty on imports
Is the most convenient duty or tax that can be collected;
One of which is, because the whole is payable
In a few places in a country, and it likewise
Operates with the greatest ease and equality,
Because as every one pays in proportion to what he consumes,
So people in general consume in proportion to what
They can afford; and therefore the tax is regulated
By the abilities which every man supposes himself
To have, or in other words, every man
Becomes his own assessor, and pays by a little at a time,
When it suits him to buy. Besides, it is a tax
Which people may pay or let alone by not consuming the articles;
And though the alternative may have no influence on their conduct,
The power of choosing is an agreeable thing to the mind.
AC-CE-248

. . . The first principle of civilization ought to have been,
And ought still to be, that the condition of every person

Born into the world after a state of civilization
commences,
Ought not to be worse than if he had been born before
that period.
But the fact is that the condition of millions,
In every country in Europe, is far worse
Than if they had been born before civilization begin,
Had been born among the Indians of North America at
the present.

AJ-332

Paine came to America at the beginnings of the Industrial Revolution. England had more sweatshops and slums, which he had seen in London.

To preserve the benefits of what is called civilized life,
And to remedy at the same time the evil which it has
produced,
Ought to considered as one of the first objects of
Reformed legislation. Whether that state that is proudly,
Perhaps erroneously, called civilization, has most
Promoted or most injured the general happiness of man
Is a question that may be strongly contested.
On one side, the spectator is dazzled by splendid appearances;
On the other, he is shocked by extremes of wretchedness;
Both of which it has erected.
The most affluent and the most miserable of the human race
Are to be found in the countries that are called civilized.
To understand what the state of society ought to be,
It is necessary to have some idea of the natural and primitive
State of man; such as it is at this day
Among the Indians of North America.
There is not, in that state, any of those spectacles
Of human misery which poverty and want present . . .
In all the towns and streets in Europe.

Poverty, therefore, is a thing created by that which is called
Civilized life. It exists not in the natural state.

On the other hand, the natural state is without those advantages
Which flow from agriculture, arts, science and manufactures.
AJ-331

This point is so obvious that it should not need stating. Yet the president, the Congress, and the Supreme Court often forget it, so it must be said. Neither the Constitution nor the government belong to any of them; both belong only to the people.

It may not be improper to observe that in both those instances
(The one of Pennsylvania, and the other of the United States),
There is no such thing as the idea of a compact
Between the people on one side, and the government on the other.
The compact was that of the people with each other,
To produce and constitute a government.
To suppose that any government can be a party
In a compact with the whole people, is to suppose it
To have existence before it can have a right to exist.
The only instance in which a compact can take place
Between the people and those who exercise the government,
Is, that the people shall pay them,
While they choose to employ them.
Government is not a trade which any man,
Or any body of men, has a right to set up
And exercise for his own emolument, but is altogether
A trust, in right of those by whom that trust is delegated,
And by whom it is always resumeable. It has
Of itself no rights; they are altogether duties.
RM-II-IV-575

When extraordinary power and extraordinary pay are allotted
To any individual in a government, he becomes the center,
Round which every kind of corruption generates and forms.
Give to any man a million a year, and add thereto the power

Of creating and disposing of places, at the expense of a
country,
And the liberties of that country are no longer secure.
What is called the splendour of a throne is no other than
The corruption of the state. It is made up of a band of
parasites,
Living in luxurious indolence, out of the public taxes.

RM-II-IV-590

Opulence is the hallmark of every dictatorship. Even if the tyrant does not engage in stealing (and many of them do), great palaces and hordes of retainers are the order of the day. There is a question of whether the "imperial presidency" in America has also moved in this dangerous direction.

Yet who, through this wilderness of error, has been to blame?
Where is the man who can say the fault, in part, has not
been his?
They were the natural, unavoidable errors of the day.
They were the errors of a whole country, which
Nothing but experience could detect and time remove.
Neither could the circumstances of America admit of system,
Till either the paper currency was fixed or laid aside.
No calculation of a finance could be made on a medium
Failing without reason, and fluctuating without rule.
But there is one error which might have been prevented
And was not; and as it is not my custom to flatter,
But to serve mankind, I will speak it freely.
It certainly was the duty of every assembly on the continent
To have known, at all times, what was the condition of its
treasury,
And to have ascertained at every period of depreciation,
How much the real worth of the taxes fell short
Of their nominal value. This knowledge,
Which might have been easily gained,
In the time of it, would have enabled them to have
Kept their constituents well informed, and this
Is one of the greatest duties of representation.
They ought to have studied and calculated
The expenses of the war, the quota of each state,

All governments owe their citizens two practical duties: one is a stable currency, the other, an honest taxation. The lack of these two things nearly caused the war to be lost and did cause the collapse of the original American government, leading to the convention to write the new constitution.

And the consequent proportion that would fall
On each man's property for his defense;
And this must have easily shown to them, that a tax
Of one hundred pounds could not be paid
By a bushel of apples or an hundred of flour,
Which was often the case two or three years ago.
But instead of this, which would have been plain
And upright dealing, the little line of temporary popularity,
The feather of an hour's duration, was too much pursued;
And in this involved condition of things, every state,
For the want of a little thinking, or a little information,
Supposed that it supported the whole expenses of the war,
When in fact it fell, by the time the tax was levied
And collected, above three-fourths short of its own quota.
CSFW-298

It is an agreeable thing to see a spirit of order and economy
Taking place, after such a series of errors and difficulties.
A government or an administration, who means and acts honestly,
Has nothing to fear, and consequently has nothing to conceal;
And it would be of use if a monthly or quarterly account
Was to be published, as well of the expenditures as of the receipts.
Eight millions of dollars must be husbanded
With an exceeding deal of care to make it do,
And, therefore, as the management must be reputable,
The publication would be serviceable.
CSFW-307

When we think or talk about taxes, we ought to recollect
That we lie down in peace and sleep in safety;
That we can follow our farms or stores or other occupations,

In prosperous tranquillity; and that these inestimable
blessings
Are procured to us by the taxes that we pay.
In this view, our taxes are properly our insurance money;
They are what we pay to be made safe, and, in strict policy,
Are the best money we can lay out.
It was my intention to offer some remarks
On the impost law of five per cent. recommended
By Congress, and to be established as a fund
For the payment of the loan-office certificates,
And other debts of the United States;
But I have already extended my piece
Beyond my intention. And as this fund will make
Our system of finance complete, and is strictly just,
And consequently requires nothing but honesty to do it,
There needs but little to be said upon it.

CSFW-307

Imagine a tax burden of only 5 percent. When the Sixteenth Amendment—to establish the income tax—was before Congress, it considered whether to cap the rate at 10 percent. Congress decided not *to do that—it did not want to encourage the federal tax rate to* rise so high. *As prophets of the future, Congress is often incompetent.*

And by a plain method of argument,
As we are running the next generation into debt,
We ought to do the work of it,
Otherwise we use them meanly and pitifully.
In order to discover the line of our duty rightly,
We should take our children in our hand,
And fix our station a few years farther into life;
That eminence will present a prospect, which
A few present fears and prejudices conceal from our sight.

CS-142

Debts we have none; and whatever we may
Contract on this account will serve as a glorious memento
Of our virtue. Can we but leave
Posterity with a settled form of government,
An independent constitution of its own,

The Balanced Budget Amendment to the Constitution would have required the federal government to balance its books each year, a requirement that many states now have. The only exceptions would have been a declaration of war or a declaration of an economic emergency by a two-thirds vote of both houses. That would have been sufficient to stop the current orgy of federal spending and deficits.

The purchase at any price will be cheap.
But to expend millions for the sake of getting a few
Vile acts repealed, and routing the present ministry only,
Is unworthy the charge, and is using posterity
With the utmost cruelty; because it is leaving them
The great work to do, and a debt upon their backs,
From which, they derive no advantage.
Such a thought is unworthy
A man of honour, and is the true characteristic
Of a narrow heart and a peddling politician.
CS-156

The logic of whether any government serves the people or harms the people is quite simple, as Paine shows. It requires what I once heard Robert Frost call "a keen eye for the obvious." What is the intent of this program? The purpose of that policy? If the purpose is seen without bias, and the results are measured, then the answer is clear whether in this instance the government serves the public well or poorly. Much of modern politics consists of deception. The purposes of programs must be misstated,

Some gentlemen have affected to call the principles
Upon which this work and the former part
Of *The Rights of Man* are founded, "a new-fangled doctrine."
The question is not whether those principles are new or old,
But whether they are right or wrong.
Suppose the former, I will show their effect
By a figure easily understood. It is now towards
The middle of February. Were I to take
A turn into the country, the trees would present
A leafless, wintery appearance. . . . By chance [I] might observe,
That a single bud on [a] twig had begun to swell.
I should reason very unnaturally, or rather not reason at all,
To suppose this was the only bud in England
Which had this appearance. Instead of
Deciding thus, I should instantly conclude,
That the same appearance was beginning, or about to begin,
Every where; and though the vegetable sleep will continue
Longer on some trees and plants than on others, and
Though some of them may not blossom for two or three years,

All will be in leaf in the summer. . . .
What pace the political summer may keep with the natural,
No human foresight can determine. It is, however,
Not difficult to perceive that the spring is begun.-
Thus wishing, as I sincerely do, freedom and happiness
To all nations, I close the SECOND PART.

RM-II-V-657

efforts to measure results must be hindered, all with the intent to maintain the status quo and to please the preferred constituency. The public is twice victimized by such politics—they do not get the benefits supposedly offered, and they pay higher taxes to support a failed program. The classic example is public education in America today. Reason is the perfect tool, the only tool, to find such answers. But reason is also very dangerous to the careers of politicians who rely on it.

There is... one point of union
wherein all religions meet.
And that is the first article
of every man's creed,
And the first of every nation
that has any creed at all.

I BELIEVE IN GOD.

Those who rest here, and
there are millions who do,
Cannot be wrong as far as
their creed goes.
Those who chuse to go further
may be wrong,
For it is impossible that
all can be right
Since there is so much
contradiction among them.

Canto VI: On Religion

THERE is . . . one point of union wherein all religions
meet
And that is the first article of every man's creed,
And the first of every nation . . . that has any creed at all.
I believe in God.
Those who rest here, and there are millions who do,
Cannot be wrong as far as their creed goes.
Those who chuse to go further may be wrong,
For it is impossible that all can be right
Since there is so much contradiction among them.

Adams-Letters-417

It has been my intention, for several years past,
To publish my thoughts upon religion. I am well aware
Of the difficulties that attend the subject, and from that
consideration,
Had reserved it to a more advanced period of life.
I intended it to be the last offering I should make
To my fellow-citizens of all nations, and that at a time
When the purity of the motive that induced me to it,
Could not admit of a question, even by
Those who might disapprove the work.

AR-I-665

Every national church or religion has established itself
By pretending some special mission from God,
Communicated to certain individuals.

Many organizations and websites either attack Paine or praise him because he is an "atheist." Early in his career, he wrote and spoke as a Christian. Later in life, he rejected all organized religions as being illogical. It was that which caused his friends and associates to condemn and reject him. But Paine was at the end a deist, not an atheist.

These two paragraphs, by themselves, sealed the fate of Paine among most of his former friends in America, in France, and in England. Though in the twentieth century, H. L. Mencken could write publicly, cheerfully, and frequently of his disbelief in all organized religions, such writings were a horror to most people in the eighteenth century, especially using the verb "pretending" with respect to Jesus Christ and all Christian churches. The last line has a very Mencken feel to it, as when he said, "Under democracy one party always devotes its chief energies to trying to prove that the other party is unfit to rule—and both commonly succeed, and are right."

Many more philosophers than Paine have struggled with the task of applying reason to religious beliefs. Most have concluded, unlike Paine, that reason is inadequate to the task, that beliefs are matters of faith, beyond the reach of logic. However, an increasing number of scientists are accepting the "deist" view of Paine, that

The Jews have
Their Moses; the Christians their Jesus Christ,
Their apostles and saints; and the Turks their Mahomet,
As if the way to God was not open to every man alike.
Each of those churches show certain books,
Which they call revelation, or the word of God.
The Jews say, that their word of God
Was given by God to Moses, face to face;
The Christians say, that their word of God
Came by divine inspiration: and the Turks say,
That their word of God (the Koran)
Was brought by an angel from Heaven.
Each of those churches accuse the other of unbelief;
And for my own part, I disbelieve them all.
AR-I-667

I know that this bold investigation will alarm many,
But it would be paying too great a compliment
To their credulity to forbear it on their account;
The times and the subject demand it to be done.
The suspicion that the theory of what is called the Christian Church
Is fabulous is becoming very extensive in all countries;
And it will be a consolation to men staggering under that suspicion,
And doubting what to believe and what to disbelieve,
To see the object freely investigated.
I therefore pass on to an examination
Of the books called the Old and New Testament.
AR-I-674

When I am told that the Koran was written in Heaven
And brought to Mahomet by an angel, the account comes
Too near the same kind of hearsay evidence

And second-hand authority as the former.
I did not see the angel myself, and,
Therefore, I have a right not to believe it.
When also I am told that a woman called the Virgin Mary,
Said, or gave out, that she was with child
Without any cohabitation with a man, and that her
betrothed husband,
Joseph, said that an angel told him so,
I have a right to believe them or not;
Such a circumstance required a much stronger evidence
Than their bare word for it;
But we have not even this—for neither Joseph nor Mary
Wrote any such matter themselves; it is only
Reported by others that *they said so*—
It is hearsay upon hearsay, and I do not
Choose to rest my belief upon such evidence.

AR-I-668

whatever one says of the doctrines of any church, the infinite complexity of the universe is a fact that bespeaks a Cause, and that Cause is the truth of God. Today that concept is called "intelligent design." It was Albert Einstein's view of the universe also.

The Christian Mythologists, after having confined Satan
In a pit, were obliged to let him out again
To bring on the sequel of the fable. He is then introduced
Into the Garden of Eden, in the shape of a snake or a
serpent,
And in that shape he enters into familiar conversation
with Eve,
Who is no way surprised to hear a snake talk;
And the issue of this tête-à-tête is that
He persuades her to eat an apple, and
The eating of that apple damns all mankind.
After giving Satan this triumph over the whole creation,
One would have supposed that the Church Mythologists
Would have been kind enough to send him back again
To the pit; or, if they had not done this,
That they would have put a mountain upon him

Paine's account of the falsity of the Christian message is akin to Mark Twain's Letters from the Earth, *a bitter satire attacking the idea of a benevolent God written after his wife and daughter had died and he had suffered other major disasters. The last part of Paine's statement, about the cruelty of God, is the same as what Twain wrote. Given the hostilities Twain expected from his book, he withheld it. It came out posthumously half a century after he wrote it.*

(For they say that their faith can remove a mountain),
Or have put him *under* a mountain, as the former mythologists
Had done, to prevent his getting again
Among the women and doing more mischief.
But instead of this they leave him at large,
Without even obliging him to give his parole—
The secret of which is, that they could not do without him;
And after being at the trouble of making him,
They bribed him to stay. They promised him
All the Jews, all the Turks by anticipation,
Nine-tenths of the world beside, and Mahomet
Into the bargain. After this, who can doubt
The bountifulness of the Christian Mythology?
Having thus made an insurrection and a battle in Heaven,
In which none of the combatants could be either killed or wounded—
Put Satan into the pit—let him out again—
Giving him a triumph over the whole creation—
Damned all mankind by the eating of an apple,
These Christian Mythologists bring the two ends
Of their fable together. They represent this
Virtuous and amiable man, Jesus Christ,
To be at once both God and Man,
And also the Son of God, celestially begotten,
On purpose to be sacrificed, because they say that
Eve in her longing had eaten an apple.
Putting aside everything that might excite laughter
By its absurdity, or detestation by its profaneness,
And confining ourselves merely to an examination of the parts,
It is impossible to conceive a story more derogatory
To the Almighty, more inconsistent with his wisdom,
More contradictory to his power, than this story is. . . .
Whenever we read the obscene stories, the voluptuous debaucheries,

The cruel and torturous executions, the unrelenting
vindictiveness,
With which more than half the Bible is filled, it would be
More consistent that we called it the word of a demon,
Than the word of God. It is a history of wickedness,
That has served to corrupt and brutalize mankind;
And, for my part, I sincerely detest it,
As I detest everything that is cruel.

AR-I-672

Revelation, when applied to religion, means something
Communicated immediately from God to man.
No one will deny or dispute the power of the Almighty
To make such a communication, if he pleases.
But admitting, for the sake of a case, that something has
been revealed
To a certain person, and not revealed to any other person,
It is revelation to that person only. When he tells it
To a second person, a second to a third, a third to a fourth,
And so on, it ceases to be a revelation to all those persons.
It is revelation to the first person only, and hearsay to
every other,
And consequently they are not obliged to believe it.
It is a contradiction in terms and ideas, to call anything
A revelation that comes to us at second-hand,
Either verbally or in writing. Revelation is necessarily
Limited to the first communication—after this,
It is only an account of something which that person says
Was a revelation made to him; and though he may find
himself
Obliged to believe it, it cannot be
Incumbent on me to believe it in the same manner;
For it was not a revelation made to me, and I have
Only his word for it that it was made to him.

AR-I-667

Paine applied pure reason to every subject that he addressed, making no exception for religion. It was his application of reason to politics that made him essential to the progress of the American Revolution. But his use of reason to dissect religion was as unwelcome in America as his attacks on monarchy made him in England.

In Paine's day, the basis of what knowledge was "correct" was in religion. Today, it is in politics and sociology. Then, the heretics were subject to burning at the stake. Today, they are subject to being denied tenure. But the process is the same and so is the harm to society. Whenever certain subjects are declared off limits, knowledge withers and is replaced by mere superstition.

So late as 1610 Galileo, a Florentine,
Discovered and introduced the use of telescopes,
And by applying them to observe the motions and appearances
Of the heavenly bodies, afforded additional means
For ascertaining the true structure of the universe.
Instead of being esteemed for these discoveries,
He was sentenced to renounce them, or the opinions
Resulting from them, as a damnable heresy.
And prior to that time, Virgilius was condemned
To be burned for asserting the antipodes, or in other words,
That the earth was a globe, and habitable in every part
Where there was land; yet the truth of this
Is now too well known even to be told. . . .
Had Newton or Descartes lived three or four hundred
Years ago, and pursued their studies as they did,
It is most probable they would not have lived
To finish them; and had Franklin drawn lightning
From the clouds at the same time, it would have
Been at the hazard of expiring for it in flames.
AR-I-698

That many good men have believed this strange fable,
And lived very good lives under that belief
(For credulity is not a crime), is what I have no doubt of.
In the first place, they were educated to believe it,
And they would have believed anything else in the same manner.
There are also many who have been so enthusiastically enraptured
By what they conceived to be the infinite love
Of God to man, in making a sacrifice of himself,
That the vehemence of the idea has forbidden and deterred them

From examining into the absurdity and profaneness of the
story.
The more unnatural anything is, the more
It is capable of becoming the object of dismal admiration.

AR-I-674

It is, however, not difficult to account for the credit
That was given to the story of Jesus Christ being
The son of God. He was born when the heathen mythology
Had still some fashion and repute in the world, and that
mythology
Had prepared the people for the belief of such a story.
Almost all the extraordinary men that lived
Under the heathen mythology were reputed to be
The sons of some of their gods. It was not a new thing,
At that time, to believe a man to have been
Celestially begotten; the intercourse of gods with women
Was then a matter of familiar opinion. Their Jupiter,
According to their accounts, had cohabited with hundreds:
The story, therefore, had nothing in it either new,
Wonderful, or obscene; it was conformable to the opinions
That then prevailed among the people called Gentiles,
Or Mythologists, and it was those people only
That believed it. The Jews who had kept strictly
To the belief of one God, and no more,
And who had always rejected the heathen
Mythology, never credited the story.

AR-I-669

This is an example of what Alexander Pope called to "damn with faint praise." Since the central belief of all Christian churches —Protestant, Catholic, and Eastern Orthodox—is the divinity of Jesus Christ, these were dangerous words, especially at a time when blasphemy was still prosecuted as a crime in America. Given that, it is amazing that The Age of Reason *was even printed. (Despite the adoption of the First Amendment, there were established churches in America; the last state to rescind its official religion was Massachusetts in 1833.)*

Nothing that is here said can apply, even with
The most distant disrespect, to the *real* character of Jesus
Christ.
He was a virtuous and an amiable man.
The morality that he preached and practiced

Was of the most benevolent kind; and though
Similar systems of morality had been preached
By Confucius, and by some of the Greek philosophers,
Many years before; by the Quakers since;
And by many good men in all ages,
It has not been exceeded by any.
AR-I-669

This is one of Paine's few reference to life after death. This was not a critical point in his theology. On the other hand, he believed in the spirit of mankind. He would have agreed with the final line of William Faulkner's Nobel Prize acceptance speech, "The poet's voice need not merely be the record of man, it can be one of the props, the pillars, to help him endure and prevail."

I trouble not myself about the manner of future existence.
I content myself with believing, even to a positive conviction,
That the power that gave me existence is able
To continue it, in any form or manner he pleases,
Either with or without this body; and it
Appears more probable to me that I shall
Continue to exist hereafter, than that
I should have had existence,
As I now have, before that existence began.
AR-I-719

It is only in the CREATION that all our ideas
And conceptions of a word of God can unite.
The Creation speaketh an universal language,
Independently of human speech or human language,
Multiplied and various as they may be.
It is an ever-existing original, which every man
Can read. It cannot be forged;
It cannot be counterfeited; it cannot be lost;
It cannot be altered; it cannot be suppressed.
It does not depend upon the will of man
Whether it shall be published or not;
It publishes itself from one end of the earth to the other.
It preaches to all nations and to all worlds;
And this word of God reveals to man
All that is necessary for man to know of God.
AR-I-687

The continually progressive change to which the
meaning
Of words is subject, the want of a universal language
Which renders translation necessary, the errors to which
Translations are again subject, the mistakes of copyists
And printers, together with the possibility of willful
alteration,
Are of themselves evidences that the human language,
Whether in speech or in print, cannot be
The vehicle of the word of God.
The word of God exists in something else.

AR-I-68C

But some, perhaps, will say: Are we to have
No word of God—no revelation? I answer,
Yes; there is a word of God; there is a revelation.
THE WORD OF GOD IS THE CREATION WE
BEHOLD
And it is in this word, which no
Human invention can counterfeit or alter,
That God speaketh universally to man.

AR-I-686

It is somewhat curious that the three persons whose
names
Are the most universally recorded, were of
Very obscure parentage. Moses was a foundling;
Jesus Christ was born in a stable; and Mahomet
Was a mule driver. The first and last of these men
Were founders of different systems of religion;
But Jesus Christ founded no new system.
He called men to the practice of moral virtues
And the belief of one God.
The great trait in his character is philanthropy.

AR-I-681

This is the one instance in Paine's work which leads to the conclusion that he misrepresented the facts in reaching his reasoned conclusion. Paine argued: "Had it been the object . . . of Jesus Christ to establish a new religion, he would undoubtedly have written the system himself, or procured it to be written *in his life time. But there is no publication extant authenticated with his name." Paine was learned enough about Moses and Muhammad to know that neither of them either wrote a single word or caused a single word to be written in their lifetimes. So in this case, Paine knew his argument was false.*

As to religion, I hold it to be the indispensable duty
Of all government, to protect all conscientious professors thereof,
And I know of no other business which government hath to do therewith.
Let a man throw aside that narrowness of soul,
That selfishness of principle, which the niggards of all professions
Are so unwilling to part with, and he will be
At once delivered of his fears on that head.
Suspicion is the companion of mean souls,
And the bane of all good society.
For myself, I fully and conscientiously believe,
That it is the will of the Almighty, that there should be
Diversity of religious opinions among us:
It affords a larger field for our Christian kindness.
Were we all of one way of thinking,
Our religious dispositions would want matter for probation;
And on this liberal principle, I look on
The various denominations among us, to be like
Children of the same family, differing only,
In what is called, their Christian names.
CS-163

Paine addressed this to certain Quakers who wrote a tract urging reconciliation with England. Often printed as an appendix to Common Sense, *this was Paine's only argument to a particular religion. Most likely, he wrote it because Quakers*

The writer of this, is one of those few, who never
Dishonours religion either by ridiculing . . . any denomination whatsoever.
To God, and not to man, are all men
Accountable on the score of religion. Wherefore,
This epistle is not so properly addressed to you as a religious,
But as a political body, dabbling in matters, which
The professed quietude of your principles instruct you not to meddle with.

. . . It is evident from the manner in which ye have managed your testimony,
That politics, (as a religious body of men) is not your proper Walk;
For however well adapted it might appear to you,
It is, nevertheless, a jumble of good and bad put unwisely together,
And the conclusion drawn therefrom, both unnatural and unjust.

CSQ-54

were prominent in Philadelphia, and because he had been raised as a Quaker in England. Now as then, religious leaders inject their opinions into matters of state. Politics and religion have never truly been separated. Nor can they ever be in a nation where men hold both with great passion. We should, as Paine did, judge the politics of the religious by the standards of logic and law, not of religion.

The inquisition in Spain does not proceed
From the religion originally professed, but from
This mule-animal, engendered between the church and the state.
The burnings in Smithfield proceeded from
The same heterogeneous production; and it was
The regeneration of this strange animal in England afterwards,
That renewed rancour and irreligion among the inhabitants,
And that drove the people called Quakers and Dissenters to America.
Persecution is not an original feature in any religion;
But it is always the strongly-marked feature
Of all law-religions, or religions established by law.
Take away the law-establishment, and every religion
Re-assumes its original benignity. In America,
A Catholic priest is a good citizen,
A good character, and a good neighbour;
An Episcopalian minister is of the same description:
And this proceeds independently of the men,
From there being no law-establishment in America.

RM-I-484

This is the true meaning of "freedom of religion"—that no religion should be preferred, not that the government should be hostile to all religion.

Paine understood the heart of freedom of conscience. If man is to be free, government must be powerless. If man is to believe and worship as he chooses, then government has no right to forbid or permit. It does not mean all should be free of the "offense" of the beliefs of others, only that government has no role. Rightly understood, that is the message of the First Amendment.

Toleration is not the opposite of Intolerance, but is the counterfeit of it.
Both are despotisms. The one assumes . . . the right of withholding
Liberty of conscience, and the other of granting it.
The one is the Pope armed with fire and faggot,
And the other is the Pope selling or granting indulgences.
The former is church and state, and the latter is church and traffic.
But Toleration may be viewed in a much stronger light.
Man worships not himself, but his Maker;
And the liberty of conscience which he claims is not for the service of himself,
But of his God. . . . Toleration, therefore, places itself,
Not between man and man, nor between church and church,
Nor between one denomination of religion and another,
But between God and man; between the being
Who worships, and the Being who is worshiped;
And by the same act of assumed authority which it tolerates
Man to pay his worship, it presumptuously and blasphemously
Sets itself up to tolerate the Almighty to receive it.
Were a bill brought into any Parliament, entitled,
"An Act to tolerate or grant liberty to the Almighty
To receive the worship of a Jew or Turk," or
"To prohibit the Almighty from receiving it,"
All men would startle and call it blasphemy.
There would be an uproar.
The presumption of toleration in religious matters
Would then present itself unmasked; but the presumption
Is not the less because the name of "Man" only appears to those laws, . . .
Mind thine own concerns.
If he believes not as thou believest, it is a proof

That thou believest not as he believes,
And . . . no earthly power can determine between you.
RM-I-482

We fight neither for revenge nor conquest;
Neither from pride nor passion;
We are not insulting the world with our fleets and armies,
Nor ravaging the globe for plunder.
Beneath the shade of our own vines are we attacked;
In our own houses, and on our own lands,
Is the violence committed against us.
We view our enemies in the character of
Highwaymen and housebreakers,
And having no defence for ourselves in the civil law,
Are obliged to punish them by the military one,
And apply the sword, in the very case,
Where you have before now, applied the halter—
Perhaps we feel for the ruined and insulted sufferers
In all and every part of the continent,
With a degree of tenderness which hath not yet made
Its way into some of your bosoms. But be ye sure
That ye mistake not the cause and ground of your testimony.
Call not coldness of soul, religion;
Nor put the Bigot in the place of the Christian.
O ye partial ministers of your own acknowledged principles.
If the bearing arms be sinful, the first going to war
Must be more so, by all the difference
Between wilful attack and unavoidable defense.
Wherefore, if ye really preach from conscience,
And mean not to make a political hobby-horse
Of your religion, convince the world thereof,
By proclaiming your doctrine to your enemies,
For they likewise bear arms. Give us proof
Of your sincerity by publishing it at St. James's,

This has always been the approach of the U.S. in war. We defeat nations, but we do not keep them and extract tribute. We do not meet the historical definition of "empire."

One need be careful in describing political protests mounted by religious leaders; most are honest, however wrong others may deem their conclusions. But some are mere hypocrites, hiding behind the cloth, demonstrating in a free society because they can, and tacitly supporting brutal tyrants because they support the politics and ignore the murders of the tyrants in whose name they demonstrate.

To the commanders in chief at Boston,
To the Admirals and Captains who are practically ravaging our coasts,
And to all the murdering miscreants who are acting
In authority under HIM whom ye profess to serve.
Had ye the honest soul of Barclay
Ye would preach repentance to your king;
Ye would tell the Royal Wretch his sins,
And warn him of eternal ruin.
Ye would not spend your partial invectives against
The injured and the insulted only, but, like faithful ministers,
Would cry aloud and spare none.
Say not that ye are persecuted, neither endeavour
To make us the authors of that reproach,
Which, ye are bringing upon yourselves;
For we testify unto all men, that we do not
Complain against you because ye are Quakers,
But because ye pretend to *be* and are *not* Quakers.
CSQ-55

It is exceedingly difficult to us to give credit
To many of your pretended scruples;
Because, we see them made by the same men,
Who, in the very instant that they are exclaiming
Against the mammon of this world, are nevertheless,
Hunting after it with a step as steady as Time,
And an appetite as keen as Death.
CSQ-57

By . . . *universal philanthropy* . . . I do not mean
Merely the sentimental benevolence of wishing well,
But the practical benevolence of doing good.
We cannot serve the Deity in the manner we serve

Those who cannot do without that service.
He needs no service from us.
We can add nothing to eternity.
But it is in our power to render a service
Acceptable to him, and that is not by praying,
But by endeavoring to make his creatures happy. . . .

The key of heaven is not in the keeping of any sect,
Nor ought the road to it be obstructed by any.
Our relation to each other in this world is as men,
And the man who is a friend to man and to his rights,
Let his religious opinions be what they may,
Is a good citizen, to whom I can give, as I ought
To do, . . . the right hand of friendship, and to none
With more hearty good will, my dear friend, than to you.
Adams-Letters-420

Paine suspected, perhaps rightly, that Samuel Adams had not read The Age of Reason *but was reacting to what others had said about that work. Thus, Paine gave a synopsis of it in his letter and emphasized what he believed, as well as disbelieved. The heart of his reply is the opening lines of this canto. Paine's attempt to mend fences with Adams, and with many others who formerly respected him and his works, was an abject failure.*

The following letter from Samuel Adams is the only passage used that is not from Paine.

"I have frequently with pleasure reflected on your services
To my native, and your adopted country.
Your *Common Sense* and your *Crisis*
Unquestionably awakened the public mind,
And led the people loudly to call for
A declaration of our national independence.
I therefore esteemed you as a war friend
To the liberty, & lasting welfare of the human race.
But when I heard, that you had turned your mind
To a defense of infidelity, I felt myself much astonished,
And more grieved, that you had attempted a measure
So injurious to the feelings, and so repugnant to the true
interest
Of so great a part of the citizens of the United States. . . .

This was the letter in which Sam Adams broke with his former friend, Tom Paine. The reference to "present President" means Jefferson, who was frequently attacked as being a "non-believer" in Christianity. This letter was published in newspapers, as was Paine's reply, which follows in part.

Our friend, the present President of the United States,
Has been calumniated for his liberal sentiments by men,
Who have attributed that liberality to a latent design
To promote the cause of infidelity. This, and
All other slanders have been made without a shadow of proof.
Neither religion, nor liberty can long subsist in the
Tumult of altercation, and amidst the noise and violence of faction.
Samuel Adams, letter to Paine, November 30, 1802
Adams-Letters-415

I received with great pleasure your . . . letter of November 30th
And I thank you also for the frankness of it.
Between men in pursuit of truth, and whose object is
The happiness of man both here and hereafter,
There ought to be no reserve.
Even error has a claim to indulgence,
If not to respect, when it is believed to be truth . . . .

I have now to inform you why I wrote [*The Age of Reason*]
And published it at the time I did.

In the first place, I saw my life in continual danger.
My friends were falling as fast as the guillotine could
Cut their heads off, and as every day I expected
The same fate, I resolved to begin my work.
I appeared to myself to be on my death bed,
For death was on every side of me. . . .

I have seen the four letters that passed between you and John Adams.
In your first letter you say, "let divines and philosophers,

statesmen and patriots, unite their endeavors
To *renovate the age* by inculcating in the minds of youth
The fear and love of the Deity, and universal philanthropy."
Why, my dear friend, this is exactly *my* religion,
And is the whole of it.
That you may have an idea that *The Age of Reason*
(For I believe you have not read it) inculcates
This reverential fear and love of the Deity,
I will give you a paragraph from it . . .

Adams-Letters-416

I believe in one God, and no more;
And I hope for happiness beyond this life.
I believe in the equality of man;
And I believe that religious duties consist
In doing justice, loving mercy, and endeavoring
To make our fellow-creatures happy.
But, lest it should be supposed that I believe
In many other things in addition to these,
I shall, in the progress of this work, declare the things
I do not believe, and my reasons for not believing them.
I do not believe in the creed professed by the Jewish church,
By the Roman church, by the Greek church,
By the Turkish church, by the Protestant church,
Nor by any church that I know of.
My own mind is my own church.
All national institutions of churches, whether Jewish,
Christian or Turkish, appear to me no other
Than human inventions, set up to terrify and enslave
Mankind, and monopolize power and profit.
I do not mean by this declaration to condemn those
Who believe otherwise; they have the same right
To their belief as I have to mine.
But it is necessary to the happiness of man, that he be

Paine wrote as a Christian early on. By the time he wrote The Age of Reason, *he was a deist, as this passage shows. He was never an atheist, as some books and websites claim with selected editing of his works.*

Mentally faithful to himself. Infidelity does not consist
In believing, or in disbelieving; it consists in professing
To believe what he does not believe.
AR-I-666

If objects for gratitude and admiration are our desire,
Do they not present themselves every hour to our eyes?
Do we not see a fair creation prepared to receive us
The instant we are born—a world furnished to our hands,
That cost us nothing? Is it we that light up the sun,
That pour down the rain, and fill the earth
With abundance? Whether we sleep or wake,
The vast machinery of the universe still goes on.
Are these things, and the blessings they indicate
In future, nothing to us? Can our gross feelings
Be excited by no other subjects than tragedy and suicide?
Or is the gloomy pride of man become so intolerable,
That nothing can flatter it but a sacrifice of the Creator? . . .
When we contemplate the immensity of that Being
Who directs and governs the incomprehensible WHOLE,
Of which the utmost ken of human sight
Can discover but a part, we ought to feel shame
At calling such paltry stories the word of God.
AR-I-674

This is the definition of "intelligent design" centuries before that concept had a name.

The only idea man can affix to the name
Of God is that of a first cause, the cause
Of all things. And incomprehensible and difficult
As it is for a man to conceive what a first cause is,
He arrives at the belief of it from the tenfold greater
Difficulty of disbelieving it. It is difficult
Beyond description to conceive that space
Can have no end; but it is
More difficult to conceive an end.
It is difficult beyond the power of man to conceive

An eternal duration of what we call time;
But it is more impossible to conceive a time
When there shall be no time.
In like manner of reasoning, everything we behold
Carries in itself the internal evidence
That it did not make itself.
Every man is an evidence to himself that he did not
Make himself; neither could his father make himself,
Nor his grandfather, nor any of his race;
Neither could any tree, plant, or animal make itself;
And it is the conviction arising from this evidence
That carries us on, as it were, by necessity
To the belief of a first cause eternally existing,
Of a nature totally different to any material existence
We know of, and by the power of which all things exist;
And this first cause man calls God.
It is only by the exercise of reason
That man can discover God.
Take away that reason, and he would be incapable
Of understanding anything; and, in this case, it would be
Just as consistent to read even the book called the Bible
To a horse as to a man. How, then, is it that
Those people pretend to reject reason? . . .
What more does man want to know than that the hand
Or power that made these things is divine,
Is omnipotent? Let him believe this with the force
It is impossible to repel, if he permits his reason to act,
And his rule of moral life will follow of course. . . .
That which is now called natural philosophy,
Embracing the whole circle of science,
Of which astronomy occupies the chief place,
Is the study of the works of God,
And of the power and wisdom of God
In his works, and is the true theology.

AR-I-687

Here is Paine's theology, the only kind which he was capable of, because it derives from reason. Paine was a deist, as was Thomas Jefferson, as was Albert Einstein, as are many of the modern scientists who investigate the far reaches of the universe and are awestruck by what they see and find. In the twenty-first century, this is an honorable position to take. That was not so in the eighteenth century. From the evidence of his writings, Paine was a deeply religious man, but not in a way that was tolerable to his times.

The system of worlds, next to us...
When we encounter a race from beyond Earth,
Our common language will be mathematics.

Canto VII: On Science & Reason

THE system of worlds, next to us
Exhibits . . . the same principles and school of science,
To the inhabitants of their systems, as our system does to us.
And in like manner through the immensity of space.
AR-I-709

Paine's conclusion was that when we meet beings from "a world beyond our own," that "our common language will be mathematics." Dr. Carl Sagan and NASA reached the same conclusion in the twentieth century, putting plaques on both Voyager *space ships that explained in mathematical terms who we were and where we are. Paine figured out that conclusion in the eighteenth century writing by candle-light with a quill pen.*

The Age of Reason by Thomas Paine
To my fellow citizens of the United States of America.

I put the following work under your protection.
It contains my opinions upon Religion.
You will do me the justice to remember,
That I have always strenuously supported the right
Of every man to his own opinion,
However different that opinion might be to mine.
He who denies to another this right, makes a slave
Of himself to his present opinion, because
He precludes himself the right of changing it.
The most formidable weapon
Against errors of every kind is Reason.
I have never used any other, and I trust I never shall.
Your affectionate friend and fellow-citizen, Thomas Paine.
AR-Introduction-665

These are the opening words of The Age of Reason, *which Paine wrote in 1794. They demonstrate the driving passion of his life.*

Perhaps the sentiments contained in the following pages,
Are not yet sufficiently fashionable to procure them
general favor;

He understood war, but was not a good soldier. He understood politics, but was no politician. Reason was his polar star, yet his application of reason to the issue of executing King Louis XVI nearly led to his execution on the guillotine. His use of reason on the Bible lost him all but a handful of friends, so he died alone and poor. Yet it was Paine's reason, unmatched by any but Jefferson, coupled with his elegant use of the English language, that make his words shine down through the years with a bright, true, and passionate flame.

The losing side in any public debate is seldom defeated outright. More often, the losing side is worn down by time and circumstance.

A long habit of not thinking a thing *wrong,*
Gives it a superficial appearance of being *right,*
And raises at first a formidable outcry in defense
Of custom. But the tumult soon subsides.
Time makes more converts than reason.
CS-115

When a man in a long cause attempts to steer his course
By anything else than some polar truth or principle,
He is sure to be lost. It is beyond the compass of his capacity
To keep all the parts of an argument together,
And make them unite in one issue, by any other means
Than having this guide always in view.
Neither memory nor invention will supply the want of it.
The former fails him, and the latter betrays him.
RM-I-511

To argue with a man who has renounced the . . . authority of reason,
And whose philosophy consists in holding humanity in contempt,
Is like administering medicine to the dead,
Or endeavoring to convert an atheist by scripture.
Enjoy, sir, your insensibility of feeling and reflecting.
It is the prerogative of animals.
And no man will envy you these honours, in which
A savage only can be your rival and a bear your master.
AC-V-151

Who the author of this production is,
Is wholly unnecessary to the public,
As the object for attention is the *doctrine itself,*
Not the *man*. Yet it may not be unnecessary
To say, that he is unconnected with any party,

And under no . . . influence public or private,
But the influence of reason and principle.
Philadelphia, February 14, 1776.

CS-Post Script-6

This is Paine's introduction of himself, at the beginning of Common Sense. *His stated task was to apply reason (or common sense) to the explanation of a nation that did not yet exist—the United States of America.*

And there is no instance, in which we have shewn less judgment,
Than in endeavouring to describe, what we call,
The ripeness or fitness of the Continent for independence.
As all men allow the measure, and vary
Only in their opinion of the time, let us,
In order to remove mistakes, take a general survey...
And endeavour, if possible, to find out the *very* time.
But we need not go far, the inquiry ceases at once,
For, the time hath found us. The general concurrence,
The glorious union of all things prove the fact.
It is not in numbers, but in unity, that our great strength lies;
Yet our present numbers are sufficient
To repel the force of all the world.

CS-155

In the following pages I offer nothing more than simple facts,
Plain arguments, and common sense;
And have no other preliminaries to settle with the reader,
Than that he will divest himself of prejudice and prepossession,
And suffer his reason and his feelings to determine for themselves;
That he will put *on,* or rather that he will not put *off,*
The true character of a man, and
Generously enlarge his views beyond the present day.

CS-136

Politics as a blood sport is infinitely complicated and irrational. But politics as the application of reason to facts—and reaching just conclusions—is quite simple. The difficulty lies in "divesting ourselves of prejudice."

This paragraph foreshadows the plot of Nineteen Eighty-Four. *The three remaining nations in the world are in continual warfare against each other, not for any reasons of international gain, but only to control their own populations. To such governments, outside enemies are essential to distract the people from seeing their real enemy, which is their own tyrannical government. If such governments lack enemies, they must create them. There is logic in permanent warfare. It is deadly, but logic nonetheless.*

As war is the system of government on the old construction,
The animosity which Nations reciprocally entertain,
Is nothing more than what the policy of their governments
Excites to keep up the spirit of the system.
Each government accuses the other
Of perfidy, intrigue, and ambition,
As a means of heating the imagination of their
Respective nations, and incensing them to hostilities.
Man is not the enemy of man,
But through the medium of a false government.
Instead, therefore, of exclaiming against the ambition of kings,
The exclamation should be directed against
The principle of such governments; and instead
Of seeking to reform the individual, the wisdom
Of a nation should apply itself to reform the system.
RM-I-539

The opinions of men with respect to government
Are changing fast in all countries.
The revolutions of America and France
Have thrown a beam of light over the world,
Which reaches into man. The enormous expense
Of governments has provoked people to think,
By making them feel; and when once the veil begins to rend,
It admits not of repair. Ignorance is of a peculiar nature:
Once dispelled, it is impossible to re-establish it.
It is not originally a thing of itself, but is only the absence of knowledge;
And though man may be *kept* ignorant,
He cannot be *made* ignorant. The mind,
In discovering truth, acts in the same manner
As it acts through the eye in discovering objects; . . .

Those who talk of a counter-revolution in France,
Show how little they understand of man.
There does not exist in the compass of language
An arrangement of words to express so much
As the means of effecting a counter-revolution.
The means must be an obliteration of knowledge;
And it has never yet been discovered how to make man
Unknow his knowledge, or unthink his thoughts.

RM-I-513

Paine was not always right. His faith in reason and the "progress" of the French blinded him to the flaws of the French Republic. When republics fail, the people usually cede power to the "man on a white horse," be he king, emperor, president for life, or merely "first among equals." The process is as old as Aristotle, as new as tomorrow's newspaper.

Of all the innocent passions which actuate the human mind
There is none more universally prevalent than curiosity.
It reaches all mankind, and in matters which concern us,
Or concern us not, it alike provokes in us a desire to know
them.

AC-X-287

It is deducible, as well from the nature of the thing
As from all the stories transmitted to us,
That the idea of landed property commenced with
cultivation,
And that there was no such thing, as landed property
before that time. . . .
There could be no such thing as landed property originally.
Man did not make the earth, and, though he had a natural
right
To occupy it, he had no right to locate as his property
In perpetuity any part of it; neither did the Creator
Of the earth open a land-office, from whence
The first title-deeds should issue.
Whence then, arose the idea of landed property?
I answer as before, that when cultivation began
The idea of landed property began with it,
From the impossibility of separating the improvement

This passage demonstrates the wide range of insight and intellect that Paine brought to any analysis. To understand any subject, he went back to first principles, or "the thing in itself," as philosophers from Plato to Kant have observed. Thus he makes the correct connection between the advent of civilization and of recorded land ownership.

Made by cultivation from the earth itself,
Upon which that improvement was made. . . .
It is only by tracing things to their origin
That we can gain rightful ideas of them,
And it is by gaining such ideas that we discover
The boundary that divides right from wrong,
And teaches every man to know his own.
I have entitled this tract "Agrarian Justice"
To distinguish it from "Agrarian Law."
AJ-333

Creative knowledge based on facts, illuminated by theories from the minds of scientists and philosophers, is not a creature confined to any nation. The study of facts and the application of logic to them may be fostered, or hindered, by a nation's culture, but such cannot be owned by any nation; they belong to a broader universe, as did Paine himself.

The soul of an islander, in its native state,
Seems bounded by the foggy confines of the water's edge,
And all beyond affords to him matters only
For profit or curiosity, not for friendship.
His island is to him his world, and fixed to that,
His every thing centers in it; while those
Who are inhabitants of a continent, by casting their eye
Over a larger field, take in likewise
A larger intellectual circuit, and thus approaching
Nearer to an acquaintance with the universe, their atmosphere
Of thought is extended, and their liberality fills a wider space.
In short, our minds seem to be measured by countries
When we are men, as they are by places when we are children,
And until something happens to disentangle us from the prejudice,
We serve under it without perceiving it.
In addition to this, it may be remarked, that men
Who study any universal science, the principles of which
Are universally known, or admitted,
And applied without distinction to the common benefit of all countries,

Obtain thereby a larger share of philanthropy
Than those who only study national arts and improvements.
Natural philosophy, mathematics and astronomy,
Carry the mind from the country to the creation,
And give it a fitness suited to the extent.
It was not Newton's honour, neither could it be his pride,
That he was an Englishman, but that he was a philosopher,
The heavens had liberated him from the prejudices of an
island,
And science had expanded his soul as boundless as his
studies.

AC-VIII-228

The internal evidence of those orations proves
To a demonstration, that the study and contemplation
Of the works of creation and the power and wisdom
Of God revealed and manifested in those works,
Made a great part of the religious devotion
Of the times in which they were written;
And it was this devotional study and contemplation
That led to the discovery of the principles upon which,
What are now called Sciences, are established;
And it is to the discovery of these principles
That almost all the Arts that contribute
To the convenience of human life, owe their existence.
Every principle art has some science for its parent,
Though the person who mechanically performs the work
Does not always, and but very seldom, perceive the
connection.
It is a fraud of the christian system to call the sciences
Human inventions; it is only the application . . . that is human.
Every science has for its basis a system
Of principles as fixed and unalterable as those
By which the universe is regulated and governed.

Paine's opening here refers to the Book of Job and the Psalms. All the giants of true science, beginning with Aristotle and ending (so far) with Stephen Hawking, have started at the same place in their inquiries as did Paine, with the universe as known to them. From this they deduce principles which, if proven, are then accepted as fact until replaced with others that better fit the observed universe.

More than all else, Paine was a philosopher, as this passage demonstrates. But he had a better ability to communicate than most other philosophers before or since.

Man cannot make principles; he can only discover them. . . .
It may be said, that man can make or draw
A triangle, and therefore a triangle is a human invention.
But the triangle, when drawn, is no other that the image
Of the principle; it is a delineation to the eye, and from thence
To the mind, of a principle that would otherwise be imperceptible.
The triangle does not make the principle,
Any more than a candle taken into a room that was dark,
Makes the chairs and tables that before were invisible. . . .
Since then man cannot make principles,
From whence did he gain a knowledge of them,
So as to be able to apply them, not only
To things on earth, but to ascertain the motions of bodies
So immensely distant from him as all the heavenly bodies are?
From whence, I ask, *could* he gain that knowledge,
But from the study of the true theology?
It is the structure of the universe that has taught this knowledge
To man. That structure is an ever existing exhibition
Of every principle upon which every part
Of mathematical science is founded.
The offspring of this science is mechanics;
For mechanics is no other that the principles of science applied. . . .

AR-I-691

The Greeks were a learned people;
But learning with them, did not consist in speaking Greek,
Any more than a Roman's speaking Latin,
Or a Frenchman's speaking French, or an Englishman . . . English.

From what we know of the Greeks, it does not appear
That they knew or studied any language but their own;
And this was one cause of their becoming so learned;
It afforded them more time to apply themselves to better
studies.
The schools of the Greeks were schools of science
And philosophy, and not of languages; and it is
In the knowledge of the things that science
And philosophy teach, that learning consists....
It would therefore be advantageous to the state of learning,
To abolish the study of dead languages, and to make
Learning consist, as it originally did, in scientific
knowledge. . . .
The human mind has a natural disposition
To scientific knowledge and the things connected with it.
The first and favorite amusement of a child,
Even before it begins to play, is that of imitating
The works of man. It builds houses with a cards or sticks;
It navigates the . . . ocean of a bowl of water with a paper
boat. . . .
It afterwards goes to school, where its genius is killed
By the barren study of a dead language,
And the philosopher is lost in the linguist.

AR-I-695

Albert Einstein and several of his biographers credit his genius to maintaining a "child's sense of wonder" throughout his adult life. Again, Paine speaks for our age, as well as for his own, in charging that schools crush the natural curiosity of children and teach them instead to be dumb, docile, and (perhaps) marginally useful to society.

Any person who has made observations on the state
And progress of the human mind, by observing his own,
Cannot but have observed that there are
Two distinct classes of what we call Thoughts;
Those that we produce in ourselves by reflection
And the act of thinking; and those that bolt into the mind
Of their own accord. I have always made it a rule
To treat those voluntary visitors with civility,
Taking care to examine, as best I was able, if they

Were worth entertaining; and it is from them
I have acquired almost all the knowledge that I have.
As to the learning that any person gains from a school . . .
It serves only, like a small capitol, to put him
In the way of beginning learning for himself afterwards.
Every person of learning is finally his own teacher;
The reason of which is, that principles,
Being of a distinct quality to circumstances,
Cannot be impressed upon the memory.
Their place of mental residence is the understanding,
And they are never so lasting as when they begin by conception.
AR-I-702

Having thus in a few words, opened the merits of the case,
I shall now proceed to the plan I have to propose,
Which is, To create a national fund, out of which
There shall be paid to every person, when arrived
At the age of twenty-one years, the sum of
Fifteen pounds sterling, as a compensation in part,
For the loss of his or her natural inheritance,
By the introduction of the system of landed property:
And also, the sum of ten pounds per annum, during life,
To every person now living, of the age of fifty years,
And to all others as they shall arrive at that age. . . .
It is proposed that the payments, as already stated,
Be made to every person, rich or poor.
It is best to make it so, to prevent invidious distinctions.
It is also right it should be so, because it is in lieu
Of the natural inheritance, which, as a right, belongs to
Every man, over and above property he may have created,
Or inherited from those who did. Such persons as do not
Choose to receive it can throw it into the common fund.
AJ-334

Paine offers here a blend of mild socialism and social security, both based on a land tax. The first was practiced in the town of Amana, Alaska, among the Indian tribes, and indirectly among all Americans. In line with its founding, all who came of age in Amana were given land for a home; all Alaskans receive annual payments from its oil revenues; all members of many Indian tribes share in the revenues of their businesses; and all Americans receive benefits indirectly from the revenues of the use of public land, paid into the general treasury. Concerning social security, since its advent under Otto von Bismarck in Germany in 1889, it has become a staple of every civilized government prosperous enough to pay the costs of the program for its elderly. On economics, as in other issues, Paine was ahead of his time.

It is not charity but a right, not bounty but justice,
That I am pleading for. The present state
Of civilization is as odious as it is unjust.
It is absolutely the opposite of what it should be,
And it is necessary that a revolution should be made in it.
The contrast of affluence and wretchedness
Continually meeting and offending the eye,
Is like dead and living bodies chained together.
Though I care as little about riches as any man,
I am a friend to riches because they are capable of good.
I care not how affluent some may be,
Provided that none be miserable in consequence of it.
But it is impossible to enjoy affluence with the felicity
It is capable of being enjoyed, while so much misery
Is mingled in the scene. The sight of the misery,
And the unpleasant sensations it suggests, which,
Though they may be suffocated cannot be extinguished,
Are a greater draw back upon the felicity of affluence
Than the proposed ten percent upon property is worth.
He that would not give the one to get rid
Of the other has no charity, even for himself.

AJ-339

The supreme irony in reading Paine's suggestion is that it has been carried out, incompetently with costs far exceeding his estimates. The funds spent to alleviate poverty have been more than enough to make all the poor members of the middle class, but instead of going to those in need, much has gone for salaries of employees in "the poverty industry." And note that the tax rate that Paine proposes to relieve the burdens on the "hereditary" poor is but 10 percent—one-fifth of current taxes.

The ascension of a man several miles high
Into the air, would have everything in it
That constitutes the idea of a miracle, if it were not
known
That a species of air can be generated several times lighter
Than the common atmospheric air, and yet possess
Elasticity enough to prevent the balloon,
In which that light air is enclosed, from being
Compressed into many times less bulk,
By the common air that surrounds it.

AR-I-714

Hydrogen is generated by electricity through water. Paine is here describing hydrogen-filled balloons, two centuries before they, and the Graf Zeppelin, *became practical. Like Leonardo da Vinci's designs for a flying machine, Paine understood the process long before most people conceived the possibility.*

Paine applied reason to the problem of durable, long-span bridges, together with his knowledge of geometry and of the properties of cast iron. From these he created the standard design iron bridge, used for two centuries until steel and cables allowed better, longer bridges. The "expert" bridge builders said he was wrong, but they were wrong, and he was right. Perhaps the last remaining iron bridge built to Paine's design is near I-81 in southern Virginia.

America abounds in rivers that interrupt
The land communication, and as by the violence of floods,
And the breaking up of the ice in the spring, the bridges,
Depending for support from the bottom of the river,
Are frequently carried away. I turned my attention,
After the revolutionary war was over, to find
A method of constructing an arch, that might,
Without rendering the height inconvenient
Or the ascent difficult, extend at once from
Shore to shore, over rivers of three, four,
Or five hundred feet and probably more. . . .

The appearances of such arches and the manner
Of forging and putting the parts together admit of many varieties,
But the principle will be the same in all.
The bridge architects I conversed with in England
Denied the principle, but it was generally supported by mathematicians,
And experiment has established the fact. . . .

My intention in presenting this memoir to Congress
Is to put the country in possession of the means
And of the right of making use of the construction freely;
As I do not intend to take any patent right for it.
COB-422

I love method, because I see and am convinced of
Its beauty and advantage. It is that
Which makes all business easy and understood, and
Without which, everything becomes embarrassed and difficult.
CSFW-305

To be happy in old age, it is necessary
That we accustom ourselves to objects that can accompany
The mind all the way through life,
And that we take the rest as good in their day.
The mere man of pleasure is miserable in old age,
And the mere drudge in business is but little better;
Whereas natural philosophy, mathematical
And mechanical science, are a continual source
Of tranquil pleasure . . . for the principles of science
Are in the creation, and are unchangeable, and of divine
origin.
Those who knew Benjamin Franklin
Will recollect that his mind was ever young;
His temper ever serene. Science, that never
Grows grey, was always his mistress.
He was never without an object;
For when we cease to have an object, we become
Like an invalid in a hospital, waiting for death.

AR-II-771

Most who study or read about the Founders of our nation know that Thomas Jefferson had an eclectic mind. He was interested in, and advanced the frontiers of, many fields of knowledge. The same was true of Ben Franklin. What few people know is that Thomas Paine had the same breadth of interest and ability.

First, canst thou by *searching* find out God?
Yes. Because, in the first place I know
I did not make myself, and yet I have existence;
And by *searching* into the nature of other things,
I find that no other thing could make itself;
And yet millions of other things exist;
Therefore it is that I know, by positive conclusion
Resulting from this search, that there is a power
Superior to all those things, and that power is God.
Secondly, Canst thou find out the Almighty
To *perfection*? No. Not only because
The power and wisdom He has manifested
In the structure of the creation that I behold,
Is to me incomprehensible, but because

Even this manifestation, great as it is,
Is probably but a small display of that
Immensity of power and wisdom by which millions
Of other worlds, to me invisible by their distance,
Were created and continue to exist.
AR-I-689

The Almighty lecturer, by displaying the principles
Of science in the structure of the universe,
Has invited man to study and to imitation.
It is as if he has said to the inhabitants of this globe
That we call ours, "I have made an earth for men
To dwell upon, and I have rendered the starry heavens
Visible, to teach him science and the arts.
He can now provide for his comfort,
And learn from my munificence to all,
To be kind to each other.
AR-I-694

**"...What we now see in the world,
From the Revolutions of America and France,
Are a revolution of the natural order of things..."**

Canto VIII: On War & Revolution

Because Paine's vision had a long reach, he understood the critical differences between these revolutions and the thousands of revolutions which had preceded them.

WHAT were formerly called Revolutions
Were little more than a change of persons,
Or an alteration of local circumstances.
They rose and fell like things, of course,
And had nothing in their existence or fate
That could influence beyond the spot that
Produced them. But what we now see in the world,
From the Revolutions of America and France,
Are a revolution in the natural order of things,
A system of principles as universal as truth
And the existence of man, and combining
Moral with political happiness and national prosperity.

RM-I-537

Those who expect to reap the blessings of freedom,
Must, like men, undergo the fatigues of supporting it.
The event of yesterday was one of those kind of alarms
Which is just sufficient to rouse us to duty,
Without being of consequence enough to depress our
fortitude.
It is not a field of a few acres of ground,
But a cause, that we are defending,
And whether we defeat the enemy in one battle,
Or by degrees, the consequences will be the same.

AC-IV-147

Minor changes in the affairs of men never justify a price paid in blood. War can only be just if it is fought for purposes both great and permanent.

. . . But if the whole continent must take up arms,
If every man must be a soldier, it is scarcely worth our while
To fight against a contemptible ministry only.
Dearly, dearly, do we pay for the repeal of the acts,
If that is all we fight for; for in a just estimation, it is
As great a folly to pay a Bunker-hill price for law, as for land.
CS-146

In this passage, Paine makes the case for a declaration of independence, not just another petition. Every just revolution warrants its own declaration of independence and declaration of its causes.

Were a manifesto to be published,
And despatched to foreign courts, setting forth
The miseries we have endured, and the peaceable methods
We have ineffectually used for redress; declaring,
At the same time, that not being able, any longer,
To live happily or safely under the cruel disposition
Of the British court, we had been driven
To the necessity of breaking off all connections with her;
At the same time, assuring all such courts
Of our peaceable disposition towards them,
And of our desire of entering into trade with them:
Such a memorial would produce more good effects to this
Continent,
Than if a ship were freighted with petitions to Britain.
CS-166

I mean not to exhibit horror for the purpose of provoking
revenge,
But to awaken us from fatal and unmanly slumbers,
That we may pursue determinately some fixed object.
It is not in the power of Britain or of Europe
To conquer America, if she do not conquer herself
By delay and timidity. The present winter is worth an age
If rightly employed, but if lost or neglected,
The whole continent will partake of the misfortune. . . .
CS-144

I should not be afraid to go with a hundred Whigs
Against a thousand Tories, were they to attempt to get
into arms.
Every Tory is a coward; for servile, slavish,
Self-interested fear is the foundation of Toryism;
And a man under such influence, though
He may be cruel, never can be brave.
But, before the line of irrecoverable separation be drawn
Between us, let us reason the matter together:
Your conduct is an invitation to the enemy,
Yet not one in a thousand of you has heart enough to join
him.
Howe is as much deceived by you as the American cause
Is injured by you. He expects you will all take up arms,
And flock to his standard, with muskets on your shoulders.
Your opinions are of no use to him,
Unless you support him personally,
For 'tis soldiers, and not Tories, that he wants.
I once felt all that kind of anger, which a man
Ought to feel, against the mean principles
That are held by the Tories: a noted one, who kept a
tavern at Amboy,
Was standing at his door, with as pretty a child in his hand,
About eight or nine years old, as I ever saw,
And after speaking his mind as freely as he thought was
prudent,
Finished with this unfatherly expression,
"Well! Give me peace in my day."
Not a man lives on the continent but fully believes
That a separation must some time or other finally take place,
And a generous parent should have said,
"If there must be trouble, let it be in my day,
That my child may have peace;"
And this single reflection, well applied,

Chamberlain returned from Munich in 1938 with a treaty signed by Hitler and announced that Britain and the world had "peace for our time." The most destructive war in history began less than a year later. A false peace does not prevent war, it only guarantees that when war comes, the enemy will have the advantage.

Is sufficient to awaken every man to duty.
AC-I-94

Though it oft does not come to light until long after, in most wars there are "back-channel communications." Paine addressed Chapter II of The American Crisis *to Lord Howe, who sought and obtained a private meeting with delegates from Congress. As usually transpires, nothing came of the meeting. Wars are not won by negotiation, but by victory alone.*

That I may not seem to accuse you unjustly,
I shall state the circumstance: by a verbal invitation of yours,
Communicated to Congress by General Sullivan,
Then a prisoner on his parole, you signified your desire
Of conferring with some members of that body as private gentlemen.
It was beneath the dignity of the American Congress
To pay any regard to a message that at best was but a genteel affront,
And had too much of the ministerial complexion
Of tampering with private persons; and which
Might probably have been the case, had the gentlemen
Who were deputed on the business possessed that kind
Of easy virtue which an English courtier is so truly distinguished by.
Your request, however, was complied with,
For honest men are naturally more tender
Of their civil than their political fame.
The interview ended as every sensible man thought it would;
For your lordship knows, as well as the writer of the Crisis,
That it is impossible for the King of England to promise
The repeal, or even the revisal of any acts of parliament;
Wherefore, on your part, you had nothing to say,
More than to request, in the room of demanding,
The entire surrender of the continent; and then,
If that was complied with, to promise that
The inhabitants should escape with their lives.
This was the upshot of the conference.
AC-II-102

. . . In war we may be certain of these two things,
Viz., that cruelty in an enemy, and motions made
With more than usual parade, are always signs of weakness.
He that can conquer, finds his mind too free and pleasant
To be brutish; and he that intends to conquer,
Never makes too much show of his strength.

We now know the enemy we have to do with.
While drunk with the certainty of victory, they disdained
To be civil; and in proportion as disappointment makes
them sober,
And their apprehensions of an European war alarm them,
They will become cringing and artful; honest they cannot
be.
But our answer to them, in either condition they may be in,
Is short and full—"As free and independent States
We are willing to make peace with you to-morrow,
But we neither can hear nor reply in any other
character."

AC-III-146

In time of war, America, or any nation, should be mindful of von Clausewitz's observation that "war is a continuation of politics by other means." When defeat of the enemy is the necessary goal, all strategies of the enemy should be ignored other than to defeat them and make them surrender. The great Chinese general Sun Tzu wrote in The Art of War *that one should always pretend the opposite of what one really plans to do.*

The British army in America care not how long
The war lasts. They enjoy an easy and indolent life.
They fatten on the folly of one country and the spoils of
another;
And, between their plunder and their prey, may go home
rich.
But the case is very different with the laboring farmer,
The working tradesman, and the necessitous poor in
England,
The sweat of whose brow goes day after day to feed,
In prodigality and sloth, the army that is robbing
Both them and us. Removed from the eye of that country
That supports them, and distant from the government

Armies in the field not only beggar those they attack, they beggar the people at home, taxed for their support. This is one more reason why war should not be lightly entered into, and once begun, prosecuted to the swiftest conclusion.

That employs them, they cut and carve for themselves,
And there is none to call them to account.
But England will be ruined, says Lord Shelburne,
If America is independent. Then I say, is England
Already ruined, for America is already independent . . .
That a nation is to be ruined by peace and commerce,
And fourteen or fifteen millions a-year less expenses
Than before, is a new doctrine in politics.
We have heard much clamor of national savings
And economy; but surely the true economy would be,
To save the whole charge of a silly, foolish,
And headstrong war; because, compared with this,
All other retrenchments are baubles and trifles.
AC-XII-342

It signifies nothing to tell us
"That the eyes of all Europe are upon us,"
Unless he hath likewise told us
What they are looking at us *for*,
Which, as he hath not done, I will:
They are looking at us, Cato, in hopes of seeing
A final separation between Britain and the Colonies,
That they, the *lookers on*, may partake of a free
And uninterrupted trade with the whole Continent of
America.
FL-I-65

There is a mystery in the countenance of some causes,
Which we have not always present judgment enough
to explain.
It is distressing to see an enemy advancing into a country,
But it is the only place in which we can beat them,
And in which we have always beaten them,
Whenever they made the attempt. The nearer

Any disease approaches to a crisis, the nearer it is to a cure.
Danger and deliverance make their advances together,
And it is only the last push, in which
One or the other takes the lead.

AC-IV-148

Lord Littleton [said], ". . . it is the principle of an
unconditional submission I would be for maintaining."
Can words be more expressive than these?
Surely the Tories will believe the Tory lords!
The truth is, they do believe them and know
As fully as any Whig on the continent knows,
That the king and ministry never had the least design
Of an accommodation with America,
But an absolute, unconditional conquest. And the part
Which the Tories were to act, was, by downright lying,
To endeavor to put the continent off its guard,
And to divide and sow discontent in the minds
Of such Whigs as they might gain an influence over.
In short, to keep up a distraction here,
That the force sent from England might . . . conquer in
"one campaign."
They and the ministry were, by a different game,
Playing into each other's hands. The cry of the Tories
In England was, "No reconciliation, no accommodation,"
In order to obtain the greater military force;
While those in America were crying nothing but
"Reconciliation and accommodation," that the force
Sent might conquer with the less resistance.

AC-III-139

Potential enemies speak with many voices, some of which contradict one another. Before entering a war and setting its goals, America—or any nation—must decide whether the enemy seeks submission or accommodation. America had one "war" with France. It involved the seizing of a few ships and the rattling of a few sabers. But because French intentions were not grossly hostile, it began without a declaration of war and ended with the signing of the Convention of Mortefontaine in 1800.

It is the violence which is done and threatened to our
persons;
The destruction of our property by an armed force;

I was out of town when I turned on my TV and saw the second plane hit the second World Trade Tower—and then the fall of both of them. I told my companion, "This means war." There are events which demand the response of war. From that point on, no arguments for negotiation by those who fear war, or dislike America itself, have any relevance. They are as worthless as the words of the Tories in the time of Paine.

The invasion of our country by fire and sword,
Which conscientiously qualifies the use of arms:
And the instant, in which such a mode of defense became necessary,
All subjection to Britain ought to have ceased;
And the independency of America, should have been considered,
As dating its era from, and published by,
The first musket that was fired against her.
This line is a line of consistency;
Neither drawn by caprice, nor extended by ambition;
But produced by a chain of events,
Of which the colonies were not the authors.
CS-Appendix-52

War consists not just of defeating the enemy, but of forcing the enemy to realize their defeat. So long as the enemy believe some kind of victory might be theirs, they will fight on. In any war, we must raise the cost of the contest until the enemy can no longer pay it. The sooner that point is reached, the sooner the war will end and peace can be established.

England finds she cannot conquer America,
And America has no wish to conquer England.
You are fighting for what you can never obtain,
And we defending what we never mean to part with.
A few words, therefore, settle the bargain.
Let England mind her own business and we will mind ours.
Govern yourselves, and we will govern ourselves.
You may then trade where you please unmolested by us,
And we will trade where we please unmolested by you;
And such articles as we can purchase of each other
Better than elsewhere may be mutually done.
If it were possible that you could carry on the war
For twenty years you must still come to this point at last . . . ,
And the sooner you think of it the better it will be for you.
AC-V-167

. . . The English fleet and army have of late gone upon
A different plan of action to what they first set out with;
For instead of going against those Colonies where

Independence prevails *most*, they go against
Those only where it prevails the *least*.
They have quitted Massachusetts . . . and gone to North
Carolina;
Supposing they had many friends there.
Why are they expected at New York? But because
They expect the inhabitants are not generally
independents,
. . . Electing the King's Attorney for a Burgess of this city,
Is a fair invitation for them to come here. . . . [Philadelphia]
FL-IV-90

Paine realized, perhaps before anyone except Washington, that the British tactics demonstrated they would not prevail. When armies fear to go into a nest of enemies, but must go where they will find "friends," they may win battles, but they must lose the war.

Suppose our armies in every part of this continent
Were immediately to disperse, every man to his home,
Or where else he might be safe, and engage
To reassemble again on a certain future day;
It is clear that you would then have no army to contend
with,
Yet you would be as much at a loss in that case
As you are now; you would be afraid
To send your troops in parties over to the continent,
Either to disarm or prevent us from assembling,
Lest they should not return; and while you kept them
together,
Having no arms of ours to dispute with,
You could not call it a conquest; you might
Furnish out a pompous page in the London Gazette
Or a New York paper, but when we
Returned at the appointed time, you would have
The same work to do that you had at first.
AC-II-112

An armed citizenry cannot be conquered. This was one of the lessons of the American Revolution. It is why the states demanded that the Second Amendment be added to the Constitution in the Bill of Rights. Switzerland has one of the highest levels of gun ownership in the world—and has been at peace for five centuries. The military tactics Paine described were shown in the movie The Patriot, *which was loosely based on the career of General Francis Marion, the "Swamp Fox," who used guerrilla tactics against the British in the South.*

Were you to obtain possession of this city,
You would not know what to do with it more than to
plunder it.

To hold it in the manner you hold New York,
Would be an additional dead weight upon your hands;
And if a general conquest is your object,
You had better be without the city than with it.
When you have defeated all our armies,
The cities will fall into your hands of themselves;
But to creep into them in the manner you got into
Princeton,
Trenton, &c. is like robbing an orchard in the night
Before the fruit be ripe, and running away in the morning.
Your experiment in the Jerseys is sufficient to teach you
That you have something more to do than barely
To get into other people's houses; and your new converts,
To whom you promised all manner of protection,
And seduced into new guilt by pardoning them
From their former virtues, must begin to have
A very contemptible opinion both of your power and
your policy.
Your authority in the Jerseys is now reduced
To the small circle which your army occupies,
And your proclamation is no where else seen
Unless it be to be laughed at.
The mighty subduers of the continent have retreated
Into a nutshell, and the proud forgivers of our sins
Are fled from those they came to pardon;
And all this at a time when they were despatching
Vessel after vessel to England with the great news of
every day.
In short, you have managed your Jersey expedition
So very dexterously, that the dead only are conquerors,
Because none will dispute the ground with them.
In all the wars which you have formerly
Been concerned in you had only armies to contend with;
In this case you have both an army and a country

To combat with. In former wars, the countries followed
The fate of their capitals; Canada fell with Quebec,
And Minorca with Port Mahon or St. Phillips;
By subduing those, the conquerors opened a way into,
And became masters of the country: here it is otherwise;
If you get possession of a city here,
You are obliged to shut yourselves up in it,
And can make no other use of it,
Than to spend your country's money in.
This is all the advantage you have drawn from New York;
And you would draw less from Philadelphia,
Because it requires more force to keep it,
And is much further from the sea. A pretty figure
You and the Tories would cut in this city,
With a river full of ice, and a town full of fire;
For the immediate consequence of your getting here
would be,
That you would be cannonaded out again,
And the Tories be obliged to make good the damage;
And this sooner or later will be the fate of New York.
I wish to see the city saved, not so much
From military as from natural motives.
'Tis the hiding place of women and children, and
Lord Howe's proper business is with our armies.
When I put all the circumstances together which ought to
be taken,
I laugh at your notion of conquering America.
Because you lived in a little country,
Where an army might run over the whole in a few days,
And where a single company of soldiers might
Put a multitude to the rout, you expected
To find it the same here. It is plain that you
Brought over with you all the narrow notions you were
bred up with,

As a matter of tactics, Paine understood the basics of guerrilla warfare better than all the British generals and equal to General Washington.

And imagined that a proclamation in the king's name
Was to do great things; but Englishmen always travel
For knowledge, and your lordship, I hope, will return,
If you return at all, much wiser than you came.
We may be surprised by events we did not expect,
And in that interval of recollection you may gain some temporary advantage:
Such was the case a few weeks ago, but we soon
Ripen again into reason, collect our strength,
And while you are preparing for a triumph,
We come upon you with a defeat.
Such it has been, and such it would be
Were you to try it a hundred times over.
Were you to garrison the places you might march over,
In order to secure their subjection,
(For remember you can do it by no other means,)
Your army would be like a stream of water running to nothing.
By the time you extended from New York to Virginia,
You would be reduced to a string of drops
Not capable of hanging together; while we,
By retreating from State to State, like a river
Turning back upon itself, would acquire strength
In the same proportion as you lost it, and
In the end be capable of overwhelming you.
The country, in the meantime, would suffer,
But it is a day of suffering, and we ought to expect it.
What we contend for is worthy the affliction we may go through.
If we get but bread to eat, and any kind of raiment to put on,
We ought not only to be contented, but thankful.
More than that we ought not to look for,
And less than that heaven has not yet suffered us to want.

He that would sell his birthright for a little salt,
Is as worthless as he who sold it for pottage without salt;
And he that would part with it for a gay coat,
Or a plain coat, ought for ever to be a slave in buff.
What are salt, sugar and finery, to the inestimable blessings
Of "Liberty and Safety!" Or what are the inconveniences
Of a few months to the tributary bondage of ages?
The meanest peasant in America, blessed with these
sentiments,
Is a happy man compared with a New York Tory;
He can eat his morsel without repining,
And when he has done, can sweeten it
With a repast of wholesome air; he can take
His child by the hand and bless it, without feeling
The conscious shame of neglecting a parent's duty.

AC-II-109

In this passage, Paine shows his understanding of the natural advantage to the Americans of their position. It is the basic tenet of guerrilla warfare to concede the cities to the enemy, hole them up there, and harass them every time they venture out until the enemy bleeds to death and is defeated. Paine understood the tactics of General Washington and why, in time, they would inevitably prevail.

. . . Until an independence is declared, the Continent
Will feel itself like a man who continues putting off
Some unpleasant business from day to day,
Yet knows it must be done, hates to set about it,
Wishes it over, and is continually haunted
With the thoughts of its necessity.

CS-167

Europe is too thickly planted with kingdoms to be long at
peace,
And whenever a war breaks out between England and
Any foreign power, the trade of America goes to ruin,
Because of her connection with Britain.
The next war may not turn out like the last,
And should it not, the advocates for reconciliation now
Will be wishing for separation then, because, neutrality
In that case, would be a safer convoy than a man of war.

The just cause of any revolution must be high, because the price of revolution is paid in blood. There is one possible exception to the rule. The fall of the Soviet Union suggests the chance that man can learn the art of revolution without a shot being fired. If Cuba becomes a free nation without warfare after Castro, there will be some hope for bloodless revolutions.

Every thing that is right or natural pleads for separation.
The blood of the slain, the weeping voice of nature cries,
'Tis time to part. Even the distance at which
The Almighty hath placed England and America,
Is a strong and natural proof, that the authority of the one,
Over the other, was never the design of Heaven.
The time likewise at which the continent was discovered,
Adds weight to the argument, and the manner
In which it was peopled increases the force of it.
The reformation was preceded by the discovery of America,
As if the Almighty graciously meant to open
A sanctuary to the persecuted in future years,
When home should afford neither friendship nor safety.
CS-141

In plain language, this is a British order to kill on capture any Americans found armed and without officers. Even under the law of war, this is barbarity. As General Sherman said, "War is hell."

In a folio general-order book belonging to Col. Rhal's battalion,
Taken at Trenton, and now in the possession of the council
Of safety for this state, the following barbarous order
Is frequently repeated, "His excellency the Commander-in-Chief orders,
That all inhabitants who shall be found with arms, not having
An officer with them, shall be immediately taken and hung up."
How many you may thus have privately sacrificed,
We know not, and the account can only be settled in another world.
AC-II-107

To be *nobly wrong* is more manly
Than to be *meanly right.*
Only let the error be disinterested—
Let it wear, *not the mask,*

But the *mark* of principle and 'tis pardonable.
It is on this large and liberal ground,
That we distinguish between men and their tenets,
And generously preserve our friendship for the one,
While we combat with every prejudice of the other.
But let not Cato take this compliment to himself;
He stands excluded from the benefit of the distinction;
He deserves it not—And if the sincerity of disdain
Can add a cubit to the stature of my sentiments,
It shall not be wanting.
It is indifferent to me who the writers of
Cato's letters are, and sufficient for me to know,
That they are gorged with absurdity, confusion,
contradiction,
And the most notorious and willful falsehoods.
Let Cato and his faction be against Independence and
welcome;
Their consequence will not *now* turn the scale:
But let them have regard to justice,
And pay some attention to the plain doctrine of reason.
Where these are wanting, the sacred cause of truth
Applauds our anger, and dignifies it with the name of
virtue.
Four letters have already appeared under
The specious name of Cato. . . .
. . . Still the writer keeps wide of the question.
Why does he thus loiter in the suburbs of the dispute?
Why hath he not shewn us what
The numerous blessings of reconciliation are,
And proved them practicable?

FL-I-60

The debate between reconciliation and independence began in the newspapers of Philadelphia, the principal challenge to Common Sense *being the letters written by Cato. Try to imagine a debate of this caliber being conducted on television today.*

A total ignorance of men lays us under
The danger of mistaking plausibility for principle.

This is one instance in which Paine flatly contradicts himself. As in Common Sense, *he claimed anonymity and said his ideas should stand for themselves. Yet, in attacking Cato he seeks to draw out the background and associations of his opponent. Paine trusted himself, but not others.*

Could the wolf bleat like the lamb,
The flock would soon be enticed into ruin;
Wherefore, to prevent the mischief, he ought to be
Seen, as well as well as *heard*. There never was,
Nor ever will be, nor ever ought to be,
Any important political debate carried on,
In which a total separation in all cases between men
And measures could be admitted with sufficient safety.
When hypocrisy shall be banished from the earth,
The knowledge of men will be unnecessary, because,
Their measures cannot then be fraudulent. . . .
We have already too much secrecy
In some things; and too little in others;
Were men more known, and measures more concealed,
We should have fewer hypocrites, and more security.
FL-II-66

From the rapid progress which America makes in every species
Of improvement, it is rational to conclude that, if the governments
Of Asia, Africa, and Europe had begun on a principle
Similar to that of America, or had not been very early
Corrupted therefrom, those countries must by this time have
Been in a far superior condition to what they are.
Age after age has passed away, for no other purpose
Than to behold their wretchedness. Could we suppose
A spectator who knew nothing of the world, and who was put into it
Merely to make his observations, he would take a great part
Of the old world to be new, just struggling with the difficulties
And hardships of an infant settlement. He could not suppose

That the hordes of miserable poor with which old
countries abound
Could be any other than those who had not yet had time
To provide for themselves. Little would he think they were
The consequence of what in such countries they call
government.
If, from the more wretched parts of the old world,
We look at those which are in an advanced stage of
improvement
We still find the greedy hand of government thrusting
Itself into every corner and crevice of industry,
And grasping the spoil of the multitude. Invention is
Continually exercised to furnish new pretenses
For revenue and taxation. It watches
Prosperity as its prey, and permits none to escape without
a tribute.
As revolutions have begun (and as the probability is always
greater
Against a thing beginning, than of proceeding after it has
begun),
It is natural to expect that other revolutions will follow.
The amazing and still increasing expenses
With which old governments are conducted,
The numerous wars they engage in or provoke,
The embarrassments they throw in the way of universal
civilization
And commerce, and the oppression and usurpation acted
at home,
Have wearied out the patience, and exhausted the property
In such a situation, and with such examples
Already existing, revolutions are to be looked for.
They are become subjects of universal conversation,
And may be considered as the order of the day.
If systems of government can be introduced

Paine considered the move to greater freedom and individual rights to be an inevitable tide in history. Sadly, two more centuries of history have shown that the opposite is true. Tyranny is still on the march. Freedom is retreating.

Less expensive and more productive
Of general happiness than those which have existed,
All attempts to oppose their progress will . . . be fruitless.
Reason, like time, will make its own way,
And prejudice will fall in a combat with interest.
If universal peace, civilization, and commerce
Are ever to be the happy lot of man, it cannot be
Accomplished but by a revolution in the system of
governments.
All the monarchical governments are military.
War is their trade, plunder and revenue their objects.
While such governments continue, peace has not the . . .
security of a day.
What is the history of all monarchical governments
But a disgustful picture of human wretchedness,
And the accidental respite of a few years' repose?
Wearied with war, and tired with human butchery,
They sat down to rest, and called it peace.
This certainly is not the condition that heaven
intended for man. . . .
The revolutions which formerly took place in the world
Had nothing in them that interested the bulk of mankind.
They extended only to a change of persons and measures,
But not of principles, and rose or fell among
The common transactions of the moment.
What we now behold may not improperly be called a
"counter-revolution."
Conquest and tyranny, at some earlier period,
Dispossessed man of his rights, and he is now recovering
them.
And as the tide of all human affairs has its ebb and flow
In directions contrary to each other, so also is it in this.
Government founded on a moral theory, on a system of
universal peace,

On the indefeasible hereditary Rights of Man,
Is now revolving from west to east by a stronger impulse
Than the government of the sword revolved from east to
 west.
It interests not particular individuals, but nations in its
 progress,
And promises a new era to the human race.

RM-II-Introduction-549

The present National Assembly of France is, strictly speaking,
The personal social compact. The members of it
Are the delegates of the nation in its original character;
Future assemblies will be the delegates of the nation
In its organized character. The authority of the present
 Assembly
Is different from what the authority of future Assemblies
 will be.
The authority of the present one is to form a constitution;
The authority of future assemblies will be to legislate
According to the principles and forms prescribed in that
 constitution;
And if experience should hereafter show that alterations,
 amendments,
Or additions are necessary, the constitution will point out
 the mode
By which such things shall be done, and not leave it
To the discretionary power of the future government.
A government on the principles on which constitutional
 governments
Arising out of society are established, cannot have the right
Of altering itself. If it had, it would be arbitrary.
It might make itself what it pleased; and wherever
Such a right is set up, it shows there is no constitution.

RM-I-469

Paine describes the authority of the Constitution and the importance of obeying its amendment clause, as did George Washington decades later in his "Farewell Address": the "Constitution which at any time exists, till changed by an explicit and authentic act of the whole people, is sacredly obligatory upon all."

The new French constitution placed the powers to declare war and to finance it exactly where the U.S. Constitution did—in the hands of elected representatives. Historians have researched all the "modern" wars (which means since 1800). Very seldom has a democracy gone to war against another democracy. This has not ended wars, for there is still an ample supply of tyrants to begin them, but it is proof that the United States and France—and Paine himself—were correct in this conclusion.

On this question of war, three things are to be considered.
First, the right of declaring it: secondly, the expense
Of supporting it: thirdly, the mode of conducting it
After it is declared. The French Constitution places the right
Where the expense must fall, and this union can only be in the nation.
The mode of conducting it after it is declared,
It consigns to the executive department. Were this the case
In all countries, we should hear but little more of wars.
RM-I-475

A continual circulation of lies among those
Who are not much in the way of hearing them contradicted,
Will in time pass for truth;
And the crime lies not in the believer but the inventor.
I am not for declaring war with every man
That appears not so warm as myself: difference of constitution,
Temper, habit of speaking, and many other things,
Will go a great way in fixing the outward character
Of a man, yet simple honesty may remain at bottom.
Some men have naturally a military turn,
And can brave hardships and the risk of life with a cheerful face;
Others have not; no slavery appears to them
So great as the fatigue of arms, and no terror
So powerful as that of personal danger.
What can we say? We cannot alter nature,
Neither ought we to punish the son
Because the father begot him in a cowardly mood.
However, I believe most men have more courage

Than they know of, and that a little at first is enough to begin with.
I knew the time when I thought that the whistling
Of a cannon ball would have frightened me almost to death;
But I have since tried it, and find that I can stand it
With as little discomposure, and, I believe,
With a much easier conscience than your lordship.

AC-II-105

It is not just in war but in a time of peace as well that the methods of propaganda and the need for courage arise in the government and among the people. Paine demonstrates here a very modern understanding of both these critical subjects in any nation.

Every thing you suffer you have sought:
Nay, had you created mischiefs on purpose to inherit them,
You could not have secured your title by a firmer deed.
The world awakens with no pity at your complaints.
You felt none for others; you deserve none for yourselves.
Nature does not interest herself in cases like yours,
But, on the contrary, turns from them with dislike,
And abandons them to punishment. You may now
Present memorials to what court you please,
But so far as America is the object, none will listen.
The policy of Europe, and the propensity there in every mind
To curb insulting ambition, and bring cruelty
To judgment, are unitedly against you;
And where nature and interest reinforce with each other,
The compact is too intimate to be dissolved. . . .
Such excesses of passionate folly, and unjust as well as
Unwise resentment, have driven you on, like Pharaoh,
To unpitied miseries, and while the importance of the quarrel
Shall perpetuate your disgrace, the flag of America
Will carry it round the world.
The natural feelings of every rational being will

In Paine's day, sketchy news traveled by horseback and in packet boats, a far cry from today's immediate reporting from the scene and TV interviews of spokesmen for all participants on global newscasts. Still, the one point is valid. The conduct of any war will be affected by world opinion of the merits of each side. Allies may quit, supplies stop, and sanctuaries close due to such opinions. Such views need tending.

Be against you, and wherever the story shall be told,
You will have neither excuse nor consolation left.
AC-VIII-224

All nations, in all wars, demonstrate "support" for their military goals. Whether such support is coerced by a dictator or freely given by the people matters not at the beginning, but is essential at the end.

The valor of a country may be learned by the bravery of its soldiery,
And the general cast of its inhabitants, but confidence of success
Is best discovered by the active measures pursued by men of property;
And when the spirit of enterprise becomes so universal as to
Act at once on all ranks of men, a war may then,
And not till then, be styled truly popular. . . . It has been
The remark of the enemy, that every thing in America
Has been done by the force of government; but when she sees individuals
Throwing in their voluntary aid, and facilitating the public measures
In concert with the established powers of the country,
It will convince her that the cause of America
Stands not on the will of a few but on the broad
Foundation of property and popularity.
AC-IX-233

"Certainly one may, with as much reason and decency,
Plead for murder, robbery, lewdness
And barbarity, as for this practice..."

Canto IX: On Slavery

CERTAINLY one may, with as much reason and
decency, Plead for murder, robbery, lewdness, and
barbarity,
As for this practice. They are not more contrary
To the natural dictates of conscience, and feelings of
humanity;
Nay, they are all comprehended in it.

AFA-8

Scholars disagree on whether Paine wrote this tract against slavery. Based on the style of this work and the timing of this, I believe it is Paine's. Ben Franklin, Dr. Benjamin Rush, and Tom Paine were all members of the first Abolitionist Society.

As these people are not convicted of forfeiting freedom,
They have still a natural, perfect right to it;
And the governments whenever they come should,
In justice set them free, and punish
Those who hold them in slavery.

AFA-7

That some desperate wretches should be willing to steal
And enslave men by violence and murder for gain,
Is rather lamentable than strange. But that many
Civilized, nay, Christianized people should approve,
And be concerned in the savage practice, is surprising;
And still persist, though it has been so often proved
Contrary to the light of nature, to every principle
Of justice and humanity, and even good policy,
By a succession of eminent men, and several late publications.

AFA-5

A few writers before Paine had condemned slavery, but none had called for its end and the punishment of its perpetrators at law. Paine was a true abolitionist.

Why is slavery included here? For two reasons: Opposition to the slave trade was entirely consistent with Paine's views on human freedom in all cases. It is also typical of Paine, having reached his conclusions, to print them, regardless of unpopularity. The text was published but without Paine's name, as with Common Sense. *The other reason to include this is that slavery yet exists in some parts of Asia and Africa, and political slavery—the ownership of human beings by the governments of their nations—yet exists on four continents.*

The managers of that trade themselves, and others,
Testify, that many of these African nation
Inhabit fertile countries, are industrious farmers,
Enjoy plenty, and lived quietly, averse to war,
Before the Europeans debauched them with liquors,
And bribing them against one another; and that
These inoffensive people are brought into slavery,
By stealing them, tempting kings to sell subjects,
Which they can have no right to do,
And hiring one tribe to war against another,
In order to catch prisoners. By such wicked
And inhuman ways the English are said to enslave
Towards one hundred thousand yearly;
Of which thirty thousand are supposed to die
By barbarous treatment in the first year; besides all
That are slain in the unnatural wars excited to take them.
So much innocent blood have the managers
And supporters of this inhuman trade to answer for
To the common Lord of all!
AFA-5

They show as little reason as conscience who put the matter by
With saying—"Men, in some cases, are lawfully
Made slaves, and why may not these?"
So men, in some cases, are lawfully put to death,
Deprived of their goods, without their consent;
May any man, therefore, be treated so,
Without any conviction of desert?
Nor is this plea mended by adding—"They are
Set forth to us as slaves, and we buy them
Without farther inquiry, let the sellers see to it."
Such men may as well join with a known band of robbers,
Buy their ill-got goods, and help on the trade;

It was the custom in Paine's day to advance all manner of arguments in favor of slavery, including those from the Bible. Paine used simple logic to attack these claims.

Ignorance is no more pleadable in one case than the other;
The sellers plainly own how they obtain them.
But none can lawfully buy without evidence
That they are not concurring with men-stealers; and as
the true owner
Has a right to reclaim his goods that were stolen, and sold;
So the slave, who is proper owner of his freedom, has
A right to reclaim it, however often sold.

AFA-6

Such arguments ill become us, since the time
Of reformation came, under gospel light.
All distinctions of nations, and privileges of one above
others,
Are ceased; Christians are taught to account all men
Their neighbors; and love their neighbors as themselves;
And do to all men as they would be done by;
To do good to all men; and man-stealing
Is ranked with enormous crimes. Is the barbarous enslaving
Our inoffensive neighbors, and treating them like wild
beasts
Subdued by force, reconcilable with all these divine
precepts?
Is this doing to them as we would desire they should do
to us.
If they could carry off and enslave some thousands of us,
Would we think it just?

AFA-7

There is a point in common for the several nations that still engage in the mass murder of humans, still engage in the subjugation of men to other men. All such nations and the few theologies that support this behavior share the claim that their victims are less than fully human, less worthy of life and liberty than they are. Absent that "justification," few men could bring themselves to engage in subjugation or mass murder of other men.

How just, how suitable to our crime is the punishment
with which
Providence threatens us? We have enslaved multitudes,
And shed much innocent blood in doing it;
And now are threatened with the same.

The paradox of America in 1776 was clear. We claimed our freedom as a right against George III, while we denied freedom to 697,697 slaves at home (according to the 1790 Census).

And while others evils are confessed, and bewailed,
Why not this especially, and publicly;
Than which no other vice, if all others,
Has brought so much guilt on the land?
AFA-8

Not until the Fourteenth Amendment was added to the Constitution in 1868 did the law guarantee for former slaves the rights of "life, liberty, [and] property" and the "equal protection of the laws."

Perhaps some could give them lands upon reasonable rent,
Some, employing them in their labor still,
Might give them some reasonable allowances for it;
So as all may have some property, and fruits of their labors
At their own disposal, and be encouraged to industry;
The family may live together, and enjoy the natural
Satisfaction of exercising relative affections and duties,
With civil protection, and other advantages, like fellow
men.
AFA-8

. . . The gain of that trade has been pursued in opposition
To the Redeemer's cause, and the happiness of men.
Are we not, therefore, bound in duty to him and to them
To repair these injuries, as far as possible,
By taking some proper measures to instruct, not only
The slaves here, but the Africans in their own countries?
Primitive Christians labored always to spread
Their divine religion; and this is equally our duty
While there is an heathen nation.
But what singular obligations
Are we under to these injured people!

These are the sentiments of JUSTICE AND
HUMANITY.
AFA-9

"The cause of America is in great measure
The cause of all mankind."

Canto X:
On the American Role

THE cause of America is in a great measure
The cause of all mankind.
Many circumstances . . . arise . . . which are not local, but
universal,
And through which the principles of all lovers of mankind
are affected,
And in the event of which, their affections are interested.
The laying of a country desolate with fire and sword,
Declaring war against the natural rights of all mankind,
And extirpating the defenders . . . from the face of the
earth,
Is the concern of every man to whom
Nature hath given the power of feeling;
Of which class, regardless of party censure, is the
Author.

CS-116

Alexander Hamilton, in the first paragraph of the Federalist *(eleven years after Paine's work), echoed the same idea: "It has been frequently remarked that it seems to have been reserved to the people of this country, by their conduct and example, to decide the important question, whether societies of men are really capable or not of establishing good government from reflection and choice, or whether they are forever destined to depend for their political constitutions on accident and force. . . . [A] wrong election of the part we shall act may, in this view, deserve to be considered as the general misfortune of mankind."*

Simple democracy was society governing itself
Without the aid of secondary means. By ingrafting
representation
Upon democracy, we arrive at a system of government
Capable of embracing and confederating all the various
Interests and every extent of territory and population;
And that also with advantages as much superior to
hereditary government,
As the republic of letters is to hereditary literature.

America serves two roles in the modern world. One is as a political model of a stable and honest government and a free and successful society and economy. Paine never imagined—or if he did, never wrote of—the fact that the strengths and resources of America could make her the strongest nation in the world. The latter was probably beyond even his imagination. He knew better than most how narrow was the victory in the Revolutionary War. Had he lived to see the War of 1812, when America barely escaped being returned to British dominion, it would have reinforced his view that America was defensible, but suggested nothing of her potential of worldwide power. Both roles are a matter of circumstance, but both are real. And they must be exercised. Unlike kings, nations have no choice of abdication from their roles in history.

It is on this system that the American government is founded.
It is representation ingrafted upon democracy
It has fixed the form by a scale parallel in all cases
To the extent of the principle. What Athens was in miniature
America will be in magnitude. The one was the wonder of the ancient world;
The other is becoming the admiration of the present.
It is the easiest of all the forms of government to be understood
And the most eligible in practice; and excludes at once
The ignorance and insecurity of the hereditary mode,
And the inconvenience of the simple democracy.
RM-II-III-567

It is in reality a self-evident position:
For no nation in a state of foreign dependence,
Limited in its commerce, and cramped and fettered in its legislative powers,
Can ever arrive at any material eminence.
America doth not yet know what opulence is;
And although the progress which she hath made stands
Unparalleled in the history of other nations,
It is but childhood, compared with what she would be capable of . . . ,
Had she, as she ought to have,
The legislative powers in her own hands.
CS-Appendix-48

The present state of America is truly alarming
To every man who is capable of reflexion.
Without law, without government, without any other mode of power
Than what is founded on, and granted by courtesy.
Held together by an unexampled concurrence of sentiment,

Which, is nevertheless subject to change,
And which, every secret enemy is endeavouring to dissolve.
Our present condition, is, Legislation without law;
Wisdom without a plan; constitution without a name;
And, what is strangely astonishing,
Perfect Independence contending for dependence.
The instance is without a precedent;
The case never existed before;
And who can tell what may be the event?

CS-Appendix-50

America's example for other nations lies not in what she has achieved, but in what she has overcome to get there. History is made of opportunities seized or lost. Shakespeare wrote of the same in Julius Caesar*: "There is a tide in the affairs of men, Which, taken at the flood, leads on to fortune" [IV, iii].*

The remembrance of those things ought to inspire us
With confidence and greatness of mind, and carry us
Through every remaining difficulty with content and
cheerfulness.
What are the little sufferings of the present day,
Compared with the hardships that are past?
There was a time, when we had neither house nor home
In safety; when every hour was the hour of alarm and
danger;
When the mind, tortured with anxiety, knew no repose,
And every thing, but hope and fortitude, was bidding us
farewell.

AC-X-292

Britain, as a nation, is, in my inmost belief,
The greatest and most ungrateful offender
Against God on the face of the whole earth.
Blessed with all the commerce she could wish for,
And furnished, by a vast extension of dominion,
With the means of civilizing both the eastern and western
world,
She has made no other use of both than proudly to idolize
Her own "thunder," and rip up the bowels of whole
countries

The world is still replete with butchers, yet most nations turn a blind eye to their depredations, either because they are led by their own butchers or because facing the truth has unpleasant consequences. Therefore, it is still the role of America to speak, and enforce, the truth about butchery.

For what she could get. Like Alexander,
She has made war her sport,
And inflicted misery for prodigality's sake.
The blood of India is not yet repaid,
Nor the wretchedness of Africa yet requited.
Of late she has enlarged her list of national cruelties
By her butcherly destruction of the Caribbs of St. Vincent's,
And returning an answer by the sword to the meek prayer
For "Peace, liberty and safety."
These are serious things, and whatever a foolish tyrant,
A debauched court, a trafficking legislature,
Or a blinded people may think, the national account
With heaven must some day or other be settled:
All countries have sooner or later been called to their reckoning;
The proudest empires have sunk when the balance
Was struck; and Britain, like an individual penitent,
Must undergo her day of sorrow, and the sooner it happens
To her the better. As I wish it over, I wish it to come,
But withal wish that it may be as light as possible.
AC-II-108

By a curious kind of revolution in accounts, the people
Of England seem to mistake their poverty for their riches;
That is, they reckon their national debt as a part of their national wealth.
They make the same kind of error which a man would do,
Who after mortgaging his estate, should add the money borrowed,
To the full value of the estate, in order to count up his worth,
And in this case he would conceive that he got rich
By running into debt. Just thus it is with England.
The government owed at the beginning of this war
One hundred and thirty-five millions sterling,

"Got rich by running into debt" has a rather modern ring to it.

And though the individuals to whom it was due
Had a right to reckon their shares as so much private
property,
Yet to the nation collectively it was so much poverty.
There are as effectual limits to public debts as to private ones,
For when once the money borrowed is so great as to
Require the whole yearly revenue to discharge the interest
thereon,
There is an end to further borrowing; in the same manner
As when the interest of a man's debts amounts to
The yearly income of his estate, there is an end to his credit.
AC-VII-200

Paine's views on the national debt are much the same as Jefferson's—necessary in times of peril, an unjust burden on posterity in times of peace. Paine also recognized the absolute limit on national debt, when interest costs alone would overwhelm current revenues. At that point, reducing the debt becomes necessary, not discretionary. Some of America's examples to the world are negative, not positive.

From a small spark, kindled in America, a flame
Has arisen not to be extinguished. . . . Man finds
Himself changed, he scarcely perceives how. He acquires
A knowledge of his rights by attending justly to his interest,
And discovers in the event that the strength and powers of
despotism
Consist wholly in the fear of resisting it,
And that, in order "*to be free, it is sufficient that he wills it.*"
RM-II-V-596

The sun never shined on a cause of greater worth.
'Tis not the affair of a city, a country, a province,
Or a kingdom, but of a continent—of at least
One eighth part of the habitable globe.
'Tis not the concern of a day, a year, or an age;
Posterity are virtually involved in the contest, and will be
More or less affected, even to the end of time,
By the proceedings now. Now is the seed time
Of continental union, faith and honour.
The least fracture now will be like a name engraved
With the point of a pin on the tender rind of a young oak;

The wound will enlarge with the tree,
And posterity read it in full grown characters.
CS-137

The first government created by immigrants to America was the Mayflower Compact. Like the Iroquois Confederation, formed between 1590 and 1605, it was an agreement among men to establish such laws and officials as they thought were necessary to their well-being. So, as Paine understood, the individuals made no compact with government. To the contrary, they created their government and retained control of it in their own hands.

It has been thought a considerable advance towards establishing
The principles of freedom to say that Government is a compact
Between those who govern and those who are governed;
But this cannot be true, because it is putting the effect before the cause;
For as man must have existed before governments existed,
There necessarily was a time when governments did not exist,
And consequently there could originally exist
No governors to form such a compact with.
The fact therefore must be that the individuals themselves,
Each in his own personal and sovereign right,
Entered into a compact with each other to produce
A government: and this is the only mode in which
Governments have a right to arise, and the only principle
On which they have a right to exist.

To possess ourselves of a clear idea of what government
Is, or ought to be, we must trace it to its origin.
In doing this we shall easily discover that governments
Must have arisen either *out* of the people or *over* the people.
Mr. Burke has made no distinction. He investigates nothing
To its source, and therefore he confounds everything;
But he has signified his intention of undertaking,
At some future opportunity, a comparison between
The constitution of England and France.

As he thus renders it a subject of controversy by
Throwing the gauntlet, I take him upon his own ground.
It is in high challenges that high truths have the right
Of appearing; and I accept it with the more readiness
because
It affords me, at the same time, an opportunity
Of pursuing the subject with respect to
Governments arising out of society.

RM-I-467

The war, on the part of America, has been a war of
natural feeling.
Brave in distress; serene in conquest; drowsy while at rest;
And in every situation generously disposed to peace;
A dangerous calm, and a most heightened zeal have,
As circumstances varied, succeeded each other.
Every passion but that of despair has been called to a tour
of duty;
And so mistaken has been the enemy, of our abilities and
disposition,
That when she supposed us conquered, we rose the
conquerors.
The extensiveness of the United States, and the variety
Of their resources; the universality of their cause,
The quick operation of their feelings,
And the similarity of their sentiments, have,
In every trying situation, produced a something,
Which, favored by providence, and pursued with ardor,
Has accomplished . . . the business of a campaign. . . .
America ever is what she thinks herself to be.
Governed by sentiment, and acting her own mind,
She becomes, as she pleases, the victor or the victim.

AC-IX-230

If America is defined by the beliefs and actions of its citizens, as Paine claims, then America, today, is in dire straits.

And by a just parity of reasoning, all Europeans meeting
In America, or any other quarter of the globe,
are countrymen;
For England, Holland, Germany, or Sweden,
When compared with the whole, stand in the same places
On the larger scale, which the divisions of street,
Town, and county do on the smaller ones;
Distinctions too limited for continental minds.
Not one third of the inhabitants, even of this province,
Are of English descent. Wherefore I reprobate the phrase
Of parent or mother country applied to England only,
As being false, selfish, narrow and ungenerous.
CS-139

Today, not even Europe is the "parent country" of America. This nation is now its own parent. This makes it all the more important that Americans understand what America is. If we lose that vision, no one can restore it.

Europe, and not England, is the parent country of
America.
This new world hath been the asylum
For the persecuted lovers of civil and religious liberty
From every part of Europe. Hither have they fled,
Not from the tender embraces of the mother, but from
The cruelty of the monster; and it is so far true of
England,
That the same tyranny which drove the first emigrants
From home, pursues their descendants still.
CS-140

Our citizenship in the United States is our national character.
Our citizenship in any particular state is only our local
distinction.
By the latter we are known at home, by the former to the
world.
Our great title is Americans—our inferior one varies with
the place.
AC-XIII-352

Our line is fixed. Our lot is cast;
And America, the child of fate, is arriving at maturity.
We have nothing to do but by a spirited and quick exertion,
To stand prepared for war or peace.
Too great to yield, and too noble to insult;
Superior to misfortune, and generous in success,
Let us untaintedly preserve the character which we have
gained,
And show to future ages an example of unequaled
magnanimity.
There is something in the cause and consequence of
America
That has drawn on her the attention of all mankind.

AC-X-291

This was a gross exaggeration when Paine wrote these words. Today it is simple truth. If the United States fails, dozens of other nations, and billions of people, will fail with us.

There is such an idea existing in the world,
As that of *national honour*, and this,
Falsely understood, is oftentimes the cause of war.
In a Christian and philosophical sense, mankind
Seem to have stood still at individual civilization,
And to retain as nations all the original rudeness of nature.
Peace by treaty is only a cessation of violence not
A reformation of sentiment. It is a substitute for a principle
That is wanting and ever will be wanting
Till the idea of national honour be rightly understood.
As individuals we profess ourselves Christians,
But as nations we are heathens, Romans, and what not. . . .
It is, I think, exceedingly easy to define
What ought to be understood by *national honour*;
For *that* which is the best character for an individual
Is the best character for a nation; and wherever
The latter exceeds or falls beneath the former,
There is a departure from the line of true greatness.

AC-VII-197

Not every "insult" to a nation is a legitimate cause for war. Some insults are richly earned, some not. There is a difference between being offended, which a great nation can wisely disregard, and being attacked, which no nation should tolerate.

Note what Paine is talking about here. In modern terms, this is "moral equivalence." Some argue that America is just like all the other nations and therefore its actions deserve no more respect than theirs. Most who would defeat America's aims do not argue that other nations are virtuous, only that America is just as bad as the rest.

But, exclusive of the wickedness, there is a personal offence
Contained in every such attempt. It is calling us
Villains: for no man asks the other to act the villain
Unless he believes him inclined to be one. . . .
Our pride is always hurt by the same propositions which
Offend our principles; for when we are shocked
At the crime, we are wounded by the suspicion of our compliance.
Could I convey a thought that might serve to regulate
The public mind, I would not make the interest
Of the alliance the basis of defending it.
All the world are moved by interest,
And it affords them nothing to boast of.
But I would go a step higher, and defend it
On the ground of honour and principle. That our public affairs
Have flourished under the alliance—that it was wisely made,
And has been nobly executed—that by its assistance
We are enabled to preserve our country from conquest,
And expel those who sought our destruction-
That it is our true interest to maintain it unimpaired,
And that while we do so no enemy can conquer us,
Are matters which experience has taught us,
And the common good of ourselves, abstracted from principles
Of faith and honour, would lead us to maintain the connection.
But over and above the mere letter of the alliance,
We have been nobly and generously treated,
And have had the same respect and attention paid to us,
As if we had been an old established country.
To oblige and be obliged is fair work among mankind,
And we want an opportunity of showing to the world that
We are a people sensible of kindness and worthy of confidence.

Character is to us, in our present circumstances, of more importance
Than interest. We are a young nation, just stepping
Upon the stage of public life, and the eye
Of the world is upon us to see how we act.
We have an enemy who is watching to destroy our reputation,
And who will go any length to gain some evidence
Against us, that may serve to render our conduct suspected,
And our character odious; because, could she accomplish this,
Wicked as it is, the world would withdraw from us,
As from a people not to be trusted,
And our task would then become difficult.

There is nothing which sets the character of a nation in a higher
Or lower light with others, than the faithfully fulfilling,
Or perfidiously breaking, of treaties.
They are things not to be tampered with:
And should Britain, which seems very probable,
Propose to seduce America into such an act of baseness,
It would merit from her some mark of unusual detestation.
It is one of those extraordinary instances in which
We ought not to be contented with the bare negative of Congress,
Because it is an affront on the multitude as well as on the government.
It goes on the supposition that the public are not honest men,
And that they may be managed by contrivance,
Though they cannot be conquered by arms.
But, let the world and Britain know, that we are neither
To be bought nor sold; that our mind is great and fixed;

Our prospect clear; and that we will support
Our character as firmly as our independence.
AC-XI-331

Individuals, or individual states, may call themselves
What they please; but the world . . . of enemies,
Is not to be held in awe by the whistling of a name.
Sovereignty must have power to protect all the parts
That compose and constitute it: and as United States
We are equal to the importance of the title, but otherwise
We are not. Our union, well and wisely regulated
And cemented, is the cheapest way of being great—
The easiest way of being powerful, and the happiest
invention
In government which the circumstances of America can
admit of.
AC-XIII-352

Paine here is answering the arguments of Karl Marx a century and a half before Marxism came into being. Yes, there must be justice for the poor, but at the same time, the rights of private property and the opportunity to work and succeed must be protected. Paine recognized what many dictators in all eras have utterly failed to understand. Destruction of property rights and

The state of civilization that has prevailed throughout
Europe,
Is as unjust in its principle, as it is horrid in its effects;
And it is the consciousness of this, and the apprehension
That such a state cannot continue when once investigation
Begins in any country, that makes the possessors
Of property dread every idea of a revolution.
It is the *hazard* and not the principle of revolutions
That retards their progress. This being the case,
It is necessary as well for the protection of property
As for the sake of justice and humanity, to form a system
That, while it preserves one part of society from
wretchedness,
Shall secure the other from depreciation.
The superstitious awe, the enslaving reverence,
That formerly surrounded affluence, is passing away

In all countries, and leaving the possessor of property
To the convulsion of accidents. When wealth and splendor,
Instead of fascinating the multitude, excite emotions of disgust;
When, instead of drawing forth admiration,
It is beheld as an insult on wretchedness; when the ostentatious appearance
It makes serves to call the right of it in question,
The case of property becomes critical, and it is only in a system
Of justice that the possessor can contemplate security.
To remove the danger, it is necessary to remove the antipathies,
And this can only be done by making property
Productive of a national blessing, extending to every individual.
When the riches of one man above another
Shall increase the national fund in the same proportion;
When it shall be seen that the prosperity of that fund
Depends on the prosperity of individuals; when the more riches
A man acquires, the better it shall for the general mass;
It is then that antipathies will cease, and property be placed
On the permanent basis of national interest and protection.

AJ-343

There are situations a nation may be in, in which peace or war,
Abstracted from every other consideration,
May be politically right or wrong.
When nothing can be lost by a war, but what must be lost
Without it, war is then the policy of that country;

stealing from the rich all that they have is not the path to well-being but the path to shared poverty and misery. The list of nations that have made this central error runs from Albania to Zimbabwe. Failed revolutions, from the First French Republic to the creation of the Soviet Union, share a fatal flaw. When they foreclose the opportunity for individual success and prosperity, they destroy the engine on which national prosperity is based. On the other hand, Paine's idea that wealth would someday excite "emotions of disgust" has not proved out. The current magazines, tabloids, and talk shows that tout the every move of the (more or less) idle rich are little different from the fascination with the doings of courts then.

Some nations "pursue self-destruction with inflexible passion." When they harm only their own citizens by brutality, it would be a harsh but logical policy to leave them alone. In the short run it seems humane to feed the starving in North Korea. But does that make sense in the long run? How long would it be before its army staged a revolt, knowing that the price of its weapons and supplies was the starvation of its family and friends? East Germany's revolt was by citizens; in North Korea, it must be the army. On the other hand, when the brutality turns against others, the world must act, which means America must act, since all international institutions are compromised by the cowardice, or brutality, of their own members.

And such was the situation of America at the commencement of hostilities:
But when no security can be gained by a war,
But what may be accomplished by a peace, the case becomes
Reversed, and such now is the situation of England.
That America is beyond the reach of conquest,
Is a fact which experience has shown and time confirmed,
And this admitted, what, I ask, is now the object
Of contention? If there be any honour
In pursuing self-destruction with inflexible passion-
If national suicide be the perfection of national glory,
You may, with all the pride of criminal happiness,
Expire unenvied and unrivaled.
AC-VIII-226

We ought to reflect, that there are three different ways,
By which an independency may hereafter be effected;
And that *one* of those *three,* will one day or other,
Be the fate of America, viz.
By the legal voice of the people in Congress;
By a military power; or by a mob:
It may not always happen that our soldiers are citizens,
And the multitude a body of reasonable men;
Virtue, as I have already remarked, is not hereditary,
Neither is it perpetual. Should an independency
Be brought about by the first of those means,
We have every opportunity and every encouragement before us,
To form the noblest purest constitution on the face of the earth.
We have it in our power to begin the world over again.

A situation, similar to the present, hath not happened
Since the days of Noah until now.
The birthday of a new world is at hand,
And a race of men, perhaps as numerous as all Europe
 contains,
Are to receive their portion of freedom from the event of
 a few months.
The Reflexion is awful—and in this point of view,
How trifling, how ridiculous, do the little, paltry
 cavellings,
Of a few weak or interested men appear,
When weighed against the business of a world.

CS-Appendix-52

The representatives of the people of France, formed into a
 National Assembly . . .
Set forth in a solemn declaration, these natural,
Imprescriptible, and inalienable rights: . . .
I. Men are born, and always continue, free and equal
In respect of their rights. Civil distinctions, therefore,
Can be founded only on public utility.
II. The end of all political associations preservation
Of the natural and imprescriptible rights of man;
And these rights are liberty, property, security and
 resistance of oppression . . .
IV. Political liberty consists in the power of doing
Whatever does not injure another.
The exercise of the natural rights of every man,
Has no other limits than those which are necessary
To secure to every other man the free exercise
Of the same rights; and these limits
Are determinable only by the law. . . .

RM-I-506

The first lesson of America to the world is this: when grievances are sufficient, governments will change. They will change by murder and mayhem or by reflection and choice; but change they will. Africa provides a textbook example of both at the border of Zimbabwe and South Africa. The first is in the middle of a bloodbath which must and will end in the death of its dictator. The second accomplished a profound change without a shot being fired when the time came.

One of the first acts of the French Assembly after it declared itself the representative of the people was to pass its "Declaration of the Rights of Man." These excerpts from that document which Paine included demonstrate both the American lineage of that document and the reasons why Paine was drawn to France, welcomed, and elected into the French Assembly. The French Revolution and its republic did not fail because of their intent, but because of their execution.

Count Vergennes resisted for a considerable time the publication
In France of American constitutions, translated into the French language:
But even in this he was obliged to give way to public opinion,
And a sort of propriety in admitting to appear what he had
Undertaken to defend. The American constitutions were to liberty
What a grammar is to language: they define its parts
Of speech, and practically construct them into syntax.
The peculiar situation of the then Marquis de la Fayette
Is another link in the great chain. He served in America
As an American officer under a commission of Congress,
And by the universality of his acquaintance was in close friendship
With the civil government of America, as well as
With the military line. He spoke the language of the country,
Entered into the discussions on the principles of government,
And was always a welcome friend at any election.
When the war closed, a vast reinforcement
To the cause of Liberty spread itself over France,
By the return of the French officers and soldiers. A knowledge
Of the practice was then joined to the theory; and all that was
Wanting to give it real existence was opportunity.
Man cannot, properly speaking, make circumstances
For his purpose, but he always has it in his power to improve them
When they occur, and this was the case in France.
RM-I-492

In a despotic government, ideas of individual freedom are like a plague that could destroy the body politic. For that reason, many modern nations would make it a crime to publish The Rights of Man *within their borders, just as England did when Part II appeared in 1792. And America is the source of this "disease" that will inevitably bring down all tyrants.*

It is a matter worthy of observation, that
The more a country is peopled, the smaller their armies are.
In military numbers, the ancients far exceeded the moderns:
And the reason is evident, for trade being the consequence
Of population, men become too much absorbed thereby
To attend to any thing else. Commerce diminishes
The spirit, both of patriotism and military defense.
And history sufficiently informs us, that the bravest
achievements
Were always accomplished in the non-age of a nation.
With the increase of commerce, England hath lost its spirit.
The city of London, notwithstanding its numbers,
Submits to continued insults with the patience of a coward.
The more men have to lose, the less willing are they to
venture.
The rich are in general slaves to fear, and submit
To courtly power with the trembling duplicity of a Spaniel.

CS-162

William Wordsworth wrote on the same theme in this couplet: "The world is too much with us; late and soon, Getting and spending, we lay waste our powers." The question for America now is whether we have become too fat, happy, and lazy either to care about our principles or defend them.

Common sense will tell us, that the power
Which hath endeavoured to subdue us, is of all others,
The most improper to defend us. Conquest may
Be effected under the pretense of friendship; and ourselves,
After a long and brave resistance, be at last cheated into
slavery.

CS-159

Paine describes the possibility that England would try to assert in peacetime the dominance over America which it lost in the Revolution. But he also describes how any powerful nation might seek to dominate a neighbor in peacetime, the leading example today being China and Taiwan.

In all my publications, where the matter would admit,
I have been an advocate for commerce, because I am
A friend to its effects. It is a pacific system, operating
To cordialise mankind, by rendering nations, as well
Individuals, useful to each other. As to the mere
Theoretical reformation, I have never preached it up.
The most effectual process is that of improving

Paine wrote at the frontiers of many disciplines, one of which was economics. It is an overstatement to say that commerce among nations will mean an end to war. There have been, and still are, many wars among nations with extensive commercial trade. Still, it is true that as nations prosper and trade increases, rational leaders of rational nations rightly conclude that they have more to gain from peace than war. Fair and open international trade is indeed an avenue to peace, but only once there no longer are any nations or leaders who will encourage wars for reasons self-destructive of them and their nations. To use an obvious example, increased trade with Nazi Germany would not have made it peaceful.

The condition of man by means of his interest;
And it is on this ground that I take my stand.
If commerce were permitted to act to the universal extent
It is capable, it would extirpate the system of war,
And produce a revolution in the uncivilized state of governments.
The invention of commerce has arisen since those governments began,
And is the greatest approach towards universal civilization
That has yet been made by any means not immediately flowing
From moral principles. Whatever has a tendency to promote
The civil intercourse of nations by an exchange of benefits,
Is a subject as worthy of philosophy as of politics.
Commerce is no other than the traffic of two individuals,
Multiplied on a scale of numbers; and by the same rule
That nature intended for the intercourse of two,
She intended that of all. For this purpose she has distributed
The materials of manufactures and commerce, in various and distant parts
Of a nation and of the world; and as they cannot be procured
By war so cheaply or so commodiously as by commerce,
She has rendered the latter the means of extirpating the former. . . .
Though the principle of all commerce is the same, the domestic,
In a national view, is the part the most beneficial;
Because the whole of the advantages, on both sides, rests
Within the nation; whereas, in foreign commerce,
It is only a participation of one-half. The most unprofitable
Of all commerce is that connected with foreign dominion.
To a few individuals it may be beneficial,
Merely because it is commerce;
But to the nation it is a loss.

The expense of maintaining dominion more than absorbs
The profits of any trade. It does not increase the general
Quantity in the world, but operates to lessen it . . . .

RM-II-V-598

If we suffer them much longer to remain among us,
We shall become as bad as themselves.
An association of vice will reduce us more than the sword.
A nation hardened in the practice of iniquity
Knows better how to profit by it,
Than a young country newly corrupted.
We are not a match for them in the line of advantageous
guilt,
Nor they for us on the principles which we bravely set out
with.
Our first days were our days of honour.
They have marked the character of America
Wherever the story of her wars are told;
And convinced of this, we have nothing to do but
Wisely and unitedly to tread the well known track.

AC-IX-232

"Universal empire is the prerogative of the writer,
His concerns are with all mankind..."

Canto XI: On Language & Poetry

UNIVERSAL empire is the prerogative of a writer.
His concerns are with all mankind,
And though he cannot command their obedience,
He can assign them their duty.
The Republic of Letters is more ancient than monarchy,
And of far higher character in the world than
The vassal court of Britain; he that rebels
Against reason is a real rebel, but he
That in defense of reason rebels against tyranny
Has a better title to "Defender of the Faith,"
Than George the Third.

AC-II-100

No student of the language—and Paine was certainly that—can avoid the temptation of the pun, especially one slyly self-promoting. Hence this aside in his address "To the People of England" in 1778.

You, gentlemen, have studied the ruin of your country,
From which it is not within your abilities to rescue her.
Your attempts to recover her are as ridiculous
As your plans which involved her are detestable.
The commissioners, being about to depart,
Will probably bring you this, and with it
My sixth number, addressed to them; and in so doing
They carry back more *Common Sense* than they brought,
And you likewise will have more than when you sent them.

AC-VII-205

Not less, I believe, than eight or ten pamphlets
Intended as answers to the former part of *The Rights of Man*

Paine was not given to self-promotion generally. Yet here he throws down the gauntlet to the opponents of his ideas on the simple grounds of success. The people of Europe, by the purchase of his work far in excess of the work of his detractors, showed their acceptance. While Paine professes humility, in fact he displays a (justified) vanity and pride.

Have been published by different persons, and not one of them
To my knowledge, has extended to a second edition,
Nor are even the titles of them so much as generally remembered.
As I am averse to unnecessary multiplying publications,
I have answered none of them. And as I believe
That a man may write himself out of reputation
When nobody else can do it,
I am careful to avoid that rock.
But as I would decline unnecessary publications on the one hand,
So would I avoid everything that might appear
Like sullen pride on the other. If Mr. Burke,
Or any person on his side on the question,
Will produce an answer to *The Rights of Man* that shall extend
To a half, or even to a fourth part of the number of copies
To which *The Rights of Man* extended, I will
Reply to his work. But until this be done,
I shall so far take the sense of the public for my guide
(And the world knows I am not a flatterer) that what they
Do not think worth while to read, is not worth mine to answer.
I suppose the number of copies to which the first part
Of *The Rights of Man* extended, taking England, Scotland
And Ireland, is not less than between forty and fifty thousand.
RM-II-Preface-543

It was the cause of America that made me an author.
The force with which it struck my mind and
The dangerous condition the country appeared to me in,
By courting an impossible and an unnatural reconciliation
With those who were determined to reduce her,

Instead of striking out into the only line that could cement
And save her, a declaration of independence,
Made it impossible for me, feeling as I did, to be silent:
And if, in the course of more than seven years,
I have rendered her any service, I have likewise
Added something to the reputation of literature,
By freely and disinterestedly employing it
In the great cause of mankind, and showing that
There may be genius without prostitution. . . .
But as the scenes of war are closed, and every man preparing
For home and happier times, I therefore take my leave of
the subject.
I have most sincerely followed it from beginning to end,
And through all its turns and windings: and whatever
country
I may hereafter be in, I shall always feel an honest pride
At the part I have taken . . . , and a gratitude
To nature and providence for putting it
In my power to be of some use to mankind.

AC-XIII-353

Mankind, as it appears to me, are always ripe enough
To understand their true interest, provided
It be presented clearly to their understanding,
And that in a manner not to create suspicion
By any thing like self-design,
Nor offend by assuming too much.
Where we would wish to reform we must not reproach.

RM-II-541

This sage advice appears in a letter to Lafayette that Paine wrote in sending him a copy of Part II of The Rights of Man. *Paine did not follow his own advice. Using language often to slash and burn, not just to inform, Paine barged through life, stating his ideas but offending his friends, and finally drove most of them away.*

Among the incivilities by which nations or individuals
provoke
And irritate each other, Mr. Burke's pamphlet
On the French Revolution is an extraordinary instance.
Neither the people of France, nor the National Assembly,

Paine was inspired to write The Rights of Man *in part by an attack on the French Revolution by Edmund Burke who had been a friend to the American Revolution. When the overthrow of monarchy was 3,000 miles away, Burke regarded it with interest. When it moved twenty-one miles away, across the English Channel, suddenly it had become too close for comfort.*

Were troubling themselves about the affairs of England,
Or the English Parliament; and that Mr. Burke should commence
An unprovoked attack upon them, both in Parliament
And in public, is a conduct that cannot be pardoned
On the score of manners, nor justified on that of policy.
There is scarcely an epithet of abuse . . . in the English language,
With which Mr. Burke has not loaded the French Nation
And the National Assembly. Everything which rancour,
Prejudice, ignorance or knowledge could suggest,
Is poured forth in the copious fury of near
Four hundred pages. In the strain and on the plan
Mr. Burke was writing, he might have written on to as many thousands.
When the tongue or the pen is let loose in a frenzy of passion,
It is the man, and not the subject, that becomes exhausted.
RM-I-435

Paine was writing to decline a request to share authorship of a publication called The Republican *in 1791. Paine declined to assist these authors because he chose to write alone. Still, these sentiments led him to France and to election into its assembly, a service that nearly ended in his execution.*

As I am a citizen of a country which knows no other Majesty
Than that of the People—no other government than
That of the representative body—no other sovereign
Than that of the Laws, and which is attached to France
Both by alliance and gratitude, I voluntarily offer you
My services in support of principles as honourable to a nation
As they are adapted to . . . the happiness of mankind.
ARep-376

For perhaps there never was a pamphlet, since the use
Of letters were known, about which so little pains were taken,

And of which so great a number went off in so short a time;
I am certain that I am within compass
When I say one hundred and twenty thousand.
The book was turned upon the world like an orphan,
To shift for itself; no plan was formed to support it,
Neither has the author ever published a syllable on the subject
From that time, till after the appearance of Cato's fourth
letter.

FL-II-67

Common Sense *was a publishing miracle. Within its first four months, a substantial portion of all literate Americans had purchased and read it. Many of those who could not read had heard it read aloud in public places. Paine knew it was a unique success, but he* underestimated *the reach of his book.*

We sometimes experience sensations
To which language is not equal.
The conception is too bulky to be born alive,
And in the torture of thinking, we stand dumb.
Our feelings, imprisoned by their magnitude,
Find no way out—and, in the struggle of expression,
Every finger tries to be a tongue. The machinery
Of the body seems too little for the mind,
And we look about for helps to show our thoughts by.
Such must be the sensation of America,
Whenever Britain, teeming with corruption,
Shall propose to her to sacrifice her faith.

AC-XI-331

Paine here presages Orwell's understanding that the corruption of our language is a necessary step in the corruption of our politics. "[T]he English language . . . becomes ugly and inaccurate because our thoughts are foolish, but the slovenliness of our language makes it easier for us to have foolish thoughts" (Orwell, Politics and the English Language, *1946).*

How easy it is to abuse truth and language,
When men, by habitual wickedness, have learned
To set justice at defiance. . . . We lament
The virtue that is debauched into a vice,
But the vice that affects a virtue becomes the more detestable:
And amongst the various assumptions of character,
Which hypocrisy has taught, and men have practiced,
There is none that raises a higher relish of disgust,
Than to see disappointed inveteracy twisting itself,
By the most visible falsehoods, into an appearance

Without freedom of the press, freedom for both the supporters of independence and its opponents, there could not have been any American Revolution. Reverence for royal symbols and the inertia of the past would have had their way. Great ideas arise in any society not just because one man thinks them—Tom Paine in Philadelphia, Sam Adams in Boston, Tom Jefferson in Virginia—but because others hear them. Suppression of the press is the first goal of all tyrants.

Of piety which it has no pretensions to.
AC-X-287

Who, Sir, hath laid any restraint on the liberty of the press?
I know of no instance, in which the press
Hath even been the object of notice, in the province,
Except on the account of the Tory letter from Kent County,
Which was published last spring in the *Pennsylvania Ledger*
Which it was the duty of every good man to detect,
Because the *honesty* of the press is as great
An object to society as the *freedom* of it.
. . . Your words are, "Nevertheless *we* submitted to it. . . ."
Who submitted, Cato, *we* Whigs or *we* Tories?
Until you clear this up, Sir,
You must content yourself with being
Ranked among the rankest of the *writing* Tories;
Because no other body of men can have any pretense
To complain of want of freedom of the press.
FL-I-62

Surprisingly, Paine never wrote about the First Amendment freedom of the press. Surely he was aware that this provision appeared first in the Virginia Bill of Rights, then in the Constitution. Perhaps the reason was that he lived *the amendment; from the beginning he wrote words that could get him*

Mankind are not now to be told they shall not think,
Or they shall not read; and publications that go no farther
Than to investigate principles of government,
To invite men to reason and reflect,
And to shew the errors and excellences of different systems,
Have a right to appear. If they do not excite attention,
They are not worth the trouble of a prosecution;
And if they do the prosecution will amount to nothing,
Since it cannot amount to a prohibition of reading.
This would be a sentence on the public, instead of the author,
And would also be the most effectual mode of . . . hastening revolutions.
RM-II-Preface-546

As the republic of letters brings forward the best
Literary productions, by giving to genius
A fair and universal chance;
So the representative system of government
Is calculated to produce the wisest laws,
By collecting wisdom from where it can be found.
I smile to myself when I contemplate
The ridiculous insignificance into which literature
And all the sciences would sink, were they made
Hereditary; and I carry the same idea into governments.
An hereditary governor is as inconsistent as an hereditary
author.
I know not whether Homer or Euclid had sons;
But I will venture an opinion that if they had,
And had left their works unfinished,
Those sons could not have completed them.

RM-II-III-563

When any necessity or occasion has pointed out the
convenience
Of addressing the public, I have never made it a
consideration
Whether the subject was popular or unpopular, but
whether
It was right or wrong; for that which is right
Will become popular, and that which is wrong,
Though by mistake it may obtain the . . . fashion of the
day,
Will soon lose the power of delusion, and sink into
disesteem.

CSFW-296

He who dares not offend cannot be honest.

FL-III-74

hanged, and his publishers risked fines and imprisonments for printing them. He assumed and used the right before it was declared.

The propensity of grooming the progeny of politicians for future office in America is most puzzling. Is it based on civic laziness that we do not care to figure out who deserves what offices? Or is it biological absurdity, the assumption that the spawn have inherited the wisdom and virtue of the originals—assuming that they had any of either to begin with? Or is it the laziness of the American press, who find it easier to cover a small group of people than a large one, and we simply have not called them on it? Both politicians and writers should be republican in their principles.

This chapter of The American Crisis *was addressed to the Earl of Carlisle, General Clinton, and William Eden, the British commissioners at New York after the U.S. treaty was signed with France. At its strongest, Tom Paine's satire against the British has a style like Mark Twain. Both understood that ridicule and humor are stronger weapons than mere logic.*

One would think that you were just awakened
From a four years' dream, and knew nothing
Of what had passed in the interval.
Is this a time to be offering pardons, or renewing
The long forgotten subjects of charters and taxation?
Is it worth your while, after every force has failed you,
To retreat under the shelter of argument and persuasion?
Or can you think that we, with nearly half your army prisoners,
And in alliance with France, are to be begged
Or threatened into submission by a piece of paper?
But as commissioners at a hundred pounds sterling a week each,
You conceive yourselves bound to do something,
And the genius of ill-fortune told you, that you must write.
For my own part, I have not put pen to paper
These several months. Convinced of our superiority
By the issue of every campaign, I was inclined to hope,
That that which all the rest of the world now see,
Would become visible to you, and therefore felt
Unwilling to ruffle your temper by fretting you
With repetitions and discoveries. There have been
Intervals of hesitation in your conduct,
From which it seemed a pity to disturb you,
And a charity to leave you to yourselves.
You have often stopped, as if you intended to think,
But your thoughts have ever been too early or too late.
AC-VI-188

All the remaining parts of the Bible, generally known
By the name of the Prophets, are the works
Of the Jewish poets and itinerant preachers,
Who mixed poetry, anecdote, and devotion together—
And those works still retain the air and style of poetry,
Though in translation.

At this point, Paine inserts a footnote that reads:

As there are many readers who do not see
That a composition is poetry unless it be in rhyme,
It is for their information that I add this note.
Poetry consists principally in two things—
Imagery and composition. The composition of poetry
Differs from that of prose in the manner of
Mixing long and short syllables together.
Take a long syllable out of a line of poetry,
And put a short one in the room of it,
Or put a long syllable where a short one should be,
And that line will lose its poetical harmony.
It will have an effect upon the line
Like that of misplacing a note in a song.
The imagery in these books, called the Prophets,
Appertains altogether to poetry. It is fictitious,
And often extravagant, and not admissible in any
Other kind of writing than poetry.
To show that these writings are composed in poetical
 numbers,
I will take ten syllables, as they stand
In the book, and make a line of the same number
Of syllables, (heroic measure) that shall rhyme
With the last word. It will then be seen
That the composition of these books is poetical measure.
The instance I shall produce is from Isaiah:

"Hear, O ye heavens, and give ear, O earth!"
'Tis God himself that calls attention forth.

Another instance I shall quote is from the mournful
 Jeremiah,
To which I shall add two other lines,

It is this passage from Paine that makes me certain that he deliberately wrote in the "heroic measure," knowing the feel, texture, and power of that style. The second proof is in his writings themselves. Page after page, line after line breaks naturally into the same heroic measure that he describes. The third proof is his references to, and quotations from, the King James Bible, Shakespeare, and Pope, all of which used the heroic measure. The fourth proof is shown by the nineteenth psalm "as paraphrased into English verse, by Addison" which he quotes from memory in The Age of Reason. *The only question is why he did not have his words typeset as lines of poetry, rather than prose. Perhaps the reason was the cost of publication—poetry occupies far more space on the page than prose. Or, skilled writer that*

For the purpose of carrying out the figure,
And showing the intention of the poet:

"O! That mine head were waters and mine eyes"
Were fountains flowing like the liquid skies;
Then would I give the mighty flood release,
And weep a deluge for the human race.

Paine's footnote on poetry ends at this point.

There is not, throughout the whole book called the Bible,
Any word that describes to us what we call a poet,
Nor any word that describes what we call poetry.
The case is, that the word prophet, to which latter times
Have affixed a new idea, was the Bible word for poet,
And the word prophesying meant the art of making poetry.
It also meant the art of playing poetry
To a tune upon any instrument of music.
We read of prophesying with pipes, tabrets, and horns—
Of prophesying with harps, with psalteries, with cymbals,
And with every other instrument of music then in fashion.
Were we now to speak of prophesying with a fiddle,
Or with a pipe and tabor, the expression would have
No meaning or would appear ridiculous,
And to some people contemptuous, because we
Have changed the meaning of the word.
We are told of Saul being among the prophets,
And also that he prophesied; but we are not told
What they prophesied, nor what he prophesied.
The case is, there was nothing to tell;
For these prophets were a company of musicians
And poets, and Saul joined in the concert,
And this was called prophesying.
The account given of this affair in the book

Called Samuel is, that Saul met a company
Of prophets; a whole company of them! Coming down
With a psaltery, a tabret, a pipe and a harp,
And that they prophesied, and that he prophesied with them.
But it appears afterward, that Saul prophesied badly;
That is, he performed his part badly;
For it is said, that an "evil spirit from God"
Came upon Saul, and he prophesied.
Now, were there no other passage in the book
Called the Bible than this, to demonstrate to us
That we have lost the original meaning of the word
Prophesy, and substituted another meaning in its place,
This alone would be sufficient;
For it is impossible to use and apply the word prophesy,
In the place it is here used and applied, if we
Give to it the sense which latter times have affixed to it.
The manner in which it is here used strips it of all
Religious meaning, and shows that a man might then be a prophet,
Or he might prophesy, as he may now be a poet or a musician,
Without any regard to the morality or immorality of his character.
The word was originally a term of science,
Promiscuously applied to poetry and to music,
And not restricted to any subject
Upon which poetry and music might be exercised.
Deborah and Barak are called prophets, not because
They predicted anything, but because they composed
The poem or song that bears their name,
In celebration of an act already done.
David is ranked among the prophets, for he was
A musician, and was also reputed to be (though perhaps very erroneously) the author of the Psalms.

he was, perhaps he concealed his poetry in the form of prose, exactly as the Bible does, leaving it to others to discover his literary secret. In Paine's footnote to the text, noted in place, he demonstrates with lines from the King James Bible how what appears to be prose is revealed as poetry by setting the lines as poetry and adding lines that rhyme with them. The editor has done the same with Paine's work, but without adding any lines of his own to prove the point.

But Abraham, Isaac, and Jacob are not called prophets;
It does not appear from any accounts we have
That they could either sing, play music, or make poetry.
We are told of the greater and the lesser prophets.
They might as well tell us of the greater
And the lesser God; for there cannot be degrees
In prophesying consistently with its modern sense.
But there are degrees in poetry, and therefore
The phrase is reconcilable to the case, when we
Understand by it the greater and the lesser poets.
AR-I-677

If I have any where expressed myself over-warmly,
'Tis from a fixed, immovable hatred I have,
And ever had, to cruel men and cruel measures.
I have likewise an aversion to monarchy,
As being too debasing to the dignity of man;
But I never troubled others with my notions till very lately,
Nor ever published a syllable in England in my life.
What I write is pure nature, and my pen and my soul
Have ever gone together. My writings
I have always given away, reserving only
The expense of printing and paper, and sometimes not even that.
I never courted either fame or interest, and my manner of life,
To those who know it, will justify what I say.
My study is to be useful, and if your lordship
Loves mankind as well as I do, you would,
Seeing you cannot conquer us, cast about
And lend your hand towards accomplishing a peace.
AC-II-115

Our very good friend the Marquis de la Fayette
Has entrusted to my care the Key to the Bastille and
A drawing, handsomely framed, representing the demolition
Of that detestable prison, as a present to your Excellency,
Of which his letter will more particularly inform.
I feel myself happy in being the person thro' whom
The Marquis has conveyed this . . . to his great Master and
Patron. . . .
That the principles of America opened the Bastille is not
To be doubted, and therefore the Key comes to the right
place.

GW-374

It is a sad indication of how far Paine fell in the esteem of his countrymen as a result of publishing his views on religion, that only four years before he'd been chosen by the Marquis de Lafayette, a hero in both the United States and France, to present the key to the Bastille to Washington, then president of the United States.

I have mentioned in the former part of *The Age of Reason*
That it had long been my intention to publish my
thoughts
Upon religion; but that I had originally reserved it
To a later period in life intending it to be the last work
I should undertake. The circumstances, however . . .
In France in the latter end of the year 1793,
Determined me to delay it no longer.
The just and humane principles of the revolution,
Which philosophy had first diffused, had been departed
from.
The idea, always dangerous to society, as it is derogatory
To the Almighty, that priests could forgive sins,
Though it seemed to exist no longer,
Had blunted the feelings of humanity, and prepared men
For the commission of all manner of crimes.
The intolerant spirit of Church persecutions had
transferred itself
Into politics; the tribunal styled revolutionary,
Supplied the place of an inquisition; and the guillotine
And the stake outdid the fire and fagot of the Church.

I saw many of my most intimate friends destroyed,
Others daily carried to prison, and I had reason to believe,
And had also intimations given me,
That the same danger was approaching myself.
Under these disadvantages, I began the former part
Of *The Age of Reason*; I had, besides, neither Bible
Nor Testament to refer to, though I was writing against both;
Nor could I procure any: notwithstanding which,
I have produced a work that no Bible believer,
Though writing at his ease, and with a library of Church books
About him, can refute. Toward the latter end of December
Of that year, a motion was made and carried,
To exclude foreigners from the convention.
There were but two in it, Anacharsis Cloots and myself;
And I saw I was particularly pointed at by Bourdon de l'Oise,
In his speech on that motion. Conceiving,
After this, that I had but a few days of liberty,
I sat down and brought the work to a close as speedily as possible;
And I had not finished it more than six hours, in the state it has since appeared,
Before a guard came there, about three in the morning, with an order
Signed by the two Committees of public Safety and Surety General
For putting me in arrestation as a foreigner,
And conveyed me to the prison of the Luxembourg.
I contrived, on my way there, to call on Joel Barlow,
And I put the manuscript of the work into his hands:
As more safe than in my possession in prison; and not knowing

What might be the fate in France either of the writer or
 the work,
I addressed it to the protection of the citizens of the
 United States. . . .
After I had been in the Luxembourg about three weeks,
The Americans then in Paris went in a body to the
 convention
To reclaim me as their countryman and friend;
But were answered by the President, Vadier,
Who was also President of the Committee of Surety-
 General,
And had signed the order for my arrestation,
That I was born in England. I heard no more,
After this, from any person out of the walls of the prison
Till the fall of Robespierre, on the 9th of Thermidor—
 July 27, 1794.
About two months before this event I was seized with a
 fever,
That in its progress had every symptom of becoming
 mortal,
And from the effects of which I am not recovered.
It was then that I remembered with renewed
 satisfaction,
And congratulated myself most sincerely,
On having written the former part of *The Age of Reason.*
I had then but little expectation of surviving,
And those about me had less. I know, therefore,
By experience, the conscientious trial of my own
 principles. . . .
I have some reason to believe, because I cannot discover
Any other cause, that this illness preserved me in existence.
Among the papers of Robespierre that were examined
And reported upon to the Convention by a Committee of
 Deputies,

Samuel Johnson once wrote, "Depend upon it, Sir, when a man knows he is to be hanged in a fortnight, it concentrates his mind wonderfully." Paine had a similar experience—his two companions were beheaded.

Paine's life was spared at the intervention of James Monroe, then ambassador to France, at the direction of Paine's friend, former secretary of state Jefferson.

Is a note in the hand-writing of Robespierre, in the
following words:
"Demander que Thomas Paine soit decrete d'accusation,
Pour l'interet de l'Amerique autant que de la France."
To demand that a decree of accusation be passed
Against Thomas Paine, for the interest of America,
As well as of France. From what cause it was
That the intention was not put in execution I know not,
And cannot inform myself, and therefore
I ascribe it to impossibility, on account of that illness.

The note from Robespierre concerning Tom Paine was a death sentence, had it been carried out. In times of grave national peril, no man can be a leader unless he has courage. Paine was not a leader of men in battle, nor a leader in government, but a leader still. Consider his courage in a cell in the Luxembourg prison. Two men imprisoned with him were fed to the guillotine; he faced the same fate himself. Yet his first concern was with his work. He had to complete his words and get them *out of prison. The cause*

The Convention, to repair as much as lay in their power
The injustice I had sustained, invited me
Publicly and unanimously to return into the Convention,
And which I accepted, to show I could bear an injury
Without permitting it to injure my principles
Or my disposition. It is not because right principles
Have been violated that they are to be abandoned.
AR-II-Preface-731

The natural bent of my mind was to science.
I had some turn, and I believe some talent,
For poetry; but this I rather repressed than encouraged,
As leading too much into the field of imagination.
As soon as I was able, I purchased a pair of globes,
And attended the philosophical lectures of Martin
and Ferguson,
And became afterwards acquainted with Dr. Bevis,
Of the society, called the Royal Society, then
Living in the Temple, and an excellent astronomer.
I had know disposition for what was called politics.
It presented to my mind no other idea than . . .
jockeyship.
When, therefore, I turned my thoughts toward matters

Of government, I had to form a system for myself,
That accorded with the moral and philosophic principles
In which I had been educated. I saw, or at least I thought I
saw,
A vast scene opening itself to the world
In the affairs of America; and it appeared to me,
That unless the Americans changed the plan they were
Then pursuing, with respect to the government of England,
And declare themselves independent, they would not only
Involve themselves in a multiplicity of new difficulties,
But shut out the prospect that was then offering itself
To mankind though their means. It was from these motives
That I published the work known . . . [as] *Common Sense*,
Which is the first work I ever did publish;
And so far as I can judge of myself,
I believe I never should have been known in the world
As an author on any subject whatsoever,
Had it not been for the affairs of America.
I wrote *Common Sense* the latter end of the year 1775,
And published it the first of January, 1776.
Independence was declared the fourth of July, following.

AR-I-701

I had no thoughts of independence or of arms.
The world could not then have persuaded me
That I should be either a soldier or an author.
If I had any talents for either, they were buried in me,
And might ever have continued so, had not the necessity
Of the times dragged and driven them into action.
I had formed my plan of life, and conceiving
Myself happy, wished every body else so.
But when the country, into which I had just set my foot,
Was set on fire about my ears, it was time to stir.
It was time for every man to stir.

was all; compared to his words, his life counted for nothing. Considering the ignominy in which he died, I hope that Paine had some vision of how his words would live on. In his own way, with his own skills, Thomas Paine was one of the greatest leaders America ever produced.

The purpose of this book is to establish two points: that Paine was one of the best analysts of politics—not meaning the getting of offices, but the study of governance—that America has ever produced with enduring results. The other purpose is to show that Paine never lost his early poetic skills, but chose a unique subject, called the United States of America.

There is no accounting for the moment of the muse when a man is compelled to take up his pen and write. Never have the times found the man more clearly than when the American Revolution gave us Paine, and he, in return, gave us a nation.

Those who had been long settled had something to defend;
Those who had just come had something to pursue;
And the call and the concern was equal and universal.
For in a country where all men were once adventurers,
The difference of a few years in their arrival
Could make none in their right.
AC-VII-194

"... America needs never be ashamed to tell her birth,
Nor relate the stages by which she rose to empire."

Canto XII: On Times to Come

IT is not every country (perhaps there is not another
In the world) that can boast so fair an origin.
Even the first settlement of America
Corresponds with the character of the revolution.
Rome, once the proud mistress of the universe,
Was originally a band of ruffians. Plunder and rapine
Made her rich, and her oppression of millions made her
great.
But America needs never be ashamed to tell her birth,
Nor relate the stages by which she rose to empire. . . .
Let, then, the world see that she can bear prosperity:
And that her honest virtue in time of peace,
Is equal to the bravest virtue in time of war. . . .
—In this situation, may she never forget that a fair
national reputation
Is of as much importance as independence.
That it possesses a charm that wins upon the world,
And makes even enemies civil. That it gives a dignity
Which is often superior to power, and
Commands reverence where pomp and splendor fail.

AC-XIII-349

It was said of Washington that he was "first in war, first in peace, first in the hearts of his countrymen." Can it be said, should it be said, that America itself is first in war, first in peace, and first in the hearts of free men, everywhere? Or has any such thought been lost in a fog of confused, or simply bad, decisions?

To reason with governments, as they have existed for ages,
Is to argue with brutes. It is only from the nations themselves
That reforms can be expected. There ought not now to
exist

Any doubt that the peoples of France, England, and America,
Enlightened and enlightening each other, shall henceforth
Be able, not merely to give the world an example of good government,
But by their united influence enforce its practice.
RMF-Preface-11

These are among the most dangerous words of Paine to the tyrants of the world, in any age. With each passing day, the means of communication expand and it becomes harder and harder to keep any peoples in ignorance of freedom. Once they know it, they will demand it, and governments will fall like the Berlin Wall ultimately did to the sledgehammers of East Germans.

The rights of men in society, are neither devisable
Nor transferable, nor annihilable, but are descendable only,
And it is not in the power of any generation to intercept
Finally, and cut off the descent. If the present generation,
Or any other, are disposed to be slaves, it does not
Lessen the right of the succeeding generation to be free.
Wrongs cannot have a legal descent.
RM-I-518

We have a perfect idea of a natural enemy
When we think of the devil, because the enmity
Is perpetual, unalterable and unabateable.
It admits, neither of peace, truce, or treaty;
Consequently the warfare is eternal, and therefore it is natural.
But man with man cannot arrange in the same opposition.
Their quarrels are accidental and equivocally created.
They become friends or enemies as the change of temper,
Or the cast of interest inclines them. . . .
If any two nations are so, then must all nations be so,
Otherwise it is not nature but custom,
And the offence frequently originates with the accuser. . . .
The expression has been often used, and always with a fraudulent design;
For when the idea of a natural enemy is conceived,
It prevents all other inquiries, and the real cause

Of the quarrel is hidden in the universality of the conceit.
Men start at the notion of a natural enemy,
And ask no other question. The cry
Obtains credit like the alarm of a mad dog,
And is one of those . . . tricks, which, by operating on the common passions,
Secures their interest through their folly.
But we, sir, are not to be thus imposed upon.
We live in a large world, and have extended
Our ideas beyond the limits and prejudices of an island.
We hold out the right hand of fellowship to all the universe. . . .

AC-VI-186

This comment foreshadows George Washington's "Farewell Address." It is the foundation of a proper foreign policy to treat fairly and openly with all nations which would do the same with us, recognizing that nations have interests, not friendships, and no hostilities are "natural" and therefore permanent. However, a hostility that is not national, but religious, may be permanent.

Alas, we have been long led away by ancient prejudices,
And made large sacrifices to superstition.
We have boasted the protection of Great-Britain, without considering,
That her motive was *interest* not *attachment;*
That she did not protect us from *our enemies* on *our account,*
But from *her enemies* on *her own account,*
From those who had no quarrel with us on any *other account,*
And who will always be our enemies on the *same account.*
Let Britain wave her pretensions to the continent,
Or the continent throw off the dependence, and we should be
At peace with France and Spain were they at war with Britain.

CS-138

Our national credo is E Pluribus Unum, *meaning "out of many [come] one." This does not mean Americans need abandon their distinct languages, religions, and cultures. Differences do not divide, so long as we recall that we are Americans first, all other things second. The great irony of the modern world is this: precisely when much of the world hungers for the stability and freedom*

. . . That a charter is to be understood as a bond of solemn obligation,
Which the whole enters into, to support the right
Of every separate part, whether of religion,

which America enjoys, we are forgetting, and losing, the very foundations of the unparalleled success of our government and society.

Paine here broaches a very modern subject. Are there times when a nation should spare the life of a former leader who has been a murderer, not necessarily for his own sake, but for the lives lost, and the damage done, as a result of his death? Corazon Aquino faced exactly that choice in allowing President Marcos, murderer of her husband, to go free, so the streets of Manila would not be awash in the blood of a war. Other nations raise the same question today.

The execution of a foreign leader for obvious crimes raises serious questions of geopolitical reality, far beyond the demerits of one man. America today faces

Personal freedom, or property. A firm bargain
And a right reckoning make long friends.
CS-164

Let then these United States be the safeguard and the asylum
Of Louis Capet. There, . . . far removed from miseries
And crimes of royalty, he may learn from the constant aspect
Of public prosperity, that the true system of government
Consists not in kings, but in fair, equal and honourable representation . . .

It has been already proposed to abolish the punishment
Of death; . . . I recollect the humane and excellent oration
Pronounced by Robespierre, on that subject, in the . . . Assembly.
PLLC-386

France has but one ally—the United States. . . .
That is the only nation which can furnish France with naval provisions,
For the kingdoms of northern Europe are, or soon will be,
At war with her. It unfortunately happens that the person
Now under discussion is considered by the Americans
As having been a friend of their revolution.
His execution will be an affliction to them,
And it is in your power not to wound the feelings of your ally.
Could I speak the French language I would descend to your bar,
And in their name become your petitioner
To respite the execution of the sentence on Louis.
PLLC-390

We may as well assert that because a child has thrived
upon milk,
That it is never to have meat, or that the first twenty years
Of our lives is to become a precedent for the next twenty.
But even this is admitting more than is true, for
I answer roundly, that America would have flourished
As much, and probably much more, had no European
power
Had any thing to do with her. The commerce,
By which she hath enriched herself are the necessaries of
life,
And will always have a market while eating is the custom
of Europe.

CS-138

questions similar to the execution of Louis XVI in 1793. It was Paine's argument in the French Assembly to spare the life of the king, along with his belief in the separation of church and state, which earned him a death sentence from Robespierre.

If there is a country in the world where concord, according
To common calculation, would be least expected,
It is America. Made up as it is of people from different
nations,
Accustomed to different forms and habits of government,
Speaking different languages, and more different in their
modes of worship,
It would appear that the union of such a people was
impracticable;
But by the simple operation of constructing government
On the principles of society and the rights of man,
Every difficulty retires, and all the parts
Are brought into cordial unison.
There the poor are not oppressed, the rich are not
privileged.
Industry is not mortified by the splendid extravagance of a
court
Rioting at its expense. Their taxes are few,
Because their government is just: and as there is nothing

Paine's warning about restricting relations with foreign nations is similar to George Washington's warning in his "Farewell Address" in 1796: "The great rule of conduct for us, in regard to foreign nations, is, in extending our commercial relations, to have with them as little political connexion as possible. So far as we have already formed engagements, let them be fulfilled with perfect good faith. Here let us stop."

America has not necessarily hewed to the path that Paine describes. When one looks at three things—1) the level of taxation; 2) the reelection rates of Congress, which mean that absent exceptionally bad behavior, they serve for life; and 3) the swarms of servants, both direct (staff) and indirect (bureaucrats)—one asks: is America coming more to resemble the Britain whose yoke she threw off, rather than the America she once was? Have our elections become so much of an inside game that lawyers and professional politicians are now our class of courtiers and "whatever [is] their rage for reformation, they carefully preserve the fraud of the profession"?

To render them wretched, there is
Nothing to engender riots and tumults.
A metaphysical man, like Mr. Burke, would have tortured
His invention to discover how such a people could be governed.
He would have supposed that some must be managed by fraud,
Others by force, and all by some contrivance;
That genius must be hired to impose upon ignorance,
And show and parade to fascinate the vulgar.
Lost in the abundance of his researches, he would have resolved
And re-resolved, and finally overlooked the plain
And easy road that lay directly before him.
One of the great advantages of the American Revolution
Has been, that it led to a discovery of the principles,
And laid open the imposition, of governments.
All the revolutions till then had been worked
Within the atmosphere of a court, and never on
The grand floor of a nation. The parties were always
Of the class of courtiers; and whatever was their rage for reformation,
They carefully preserved the fraud of the profession.
In all cases they took care to represent government
As a thing made up of mysteries, which only themselves
Understood; and they hid from the understanding of the nation
The only thing that was beneficial to know, namely,
That government is nothing more than
A national association adding on the principles of society.
RM-II-I-554

The independence of America, considered merely as
A separation from England, would have been a matter

But of little importance, had it not been accompanied by a
revolution
In the principles and practice of governments.
She made a stand, not for herself only, but for the world,
And looked beyond the advantages herself could receive.
Even the Hessian, though hired to fight against her,
May live to bless his defeat; and England, condemning the
Viciousness of its government, rejoice in its miscarriage.
As America was the only spot in the political world
Where the principle of universal reformation could begin,
So also was it the best in the natural world. An assemblage
Of circumstances conspired, not only to give birth,
But to add gigantic maturity to its principles.
RM-II-Introduction-548

. . . Our duty to mankind at large, as well as to ourselves,
Instruct us to renounce the alliance: Because,
Any submission to, or dependence on Great Britain,
Tends directly to involve this continent in European wars
And quarrels; and sets us at variance with nations,
Who would otherwise seek our friendship,
And against whom, we have neither anger nor complaint.
CS-141

But the most offensive falsehood in the paragraph is
The attributing the prosperity of America to a wrong
cause.
It was the unremitted industry of the settlers and their
descendants,
The hard labor and toil of persevering fortitude,
That were the true causes of the prosperity of America.
The former tyranny of England served to people it,
And the virtue of the adventurers to improve it.
Ask the man, who, with his axe, has cleared

This was part of Paine's response to the speech from King George III. America leads the world in two ways—the first is political freedom and the rights of men. The second is closely related—economic freedom. As Paine correctly observed two centuries ago, free men in a free economy are an engine of success, unparalleled in the world. To the extent that other nations fail to give their citizens and their markets freedom to act, they will fail to prosper, blame others, and seek handouts. Readers can choose their own examples around the globe. Or these days, choose bad examples from within the United States.

A way in the wilderness, and now possesses an estate,
What made him rich, and he will tell you
The labor of his hands, the sweat of his brow,
And the blessing of heaven. Let Britain but leave
America to herself and she asks no more.
She has risen into greatness without the knowledge
And against the will of England, and has a right
To the unmolested enjoyment of her own created wealth.
AC-X-290

Wherefore, we never can be more capable to begin on
Maritime matters than now, while our timber is standing,
Our fisheries blocked up, and our sailors and shipwrights
out of employ.
Men of war, of seventy and eighty guns were built forty
years ago
In New-England, and why not the same now?
Ship-building is America's greatest pride,
And in which, she will in time excel the whole world.
The great empires of the east are mostly inland,
And consequently excluded from the possibility of rivaling
her.
Africa is in a state of barbarism; and no power in Europe,
Hath either such an extent of coast,
Or such an internal supply of materials.
Where nature hath given the one, she has withheld the other;
To America only hath she been liberal of both.
The vast empire of Russia is almost shut out
From the sea; . . . her boundless forests, her tar,
Iron, and cordage are only articles of commerce.
CS-159

Navies were the heart of warfare in Paine's day. The first cabinet under Washington had no secretary of defense, or army, only the navy. Today, dominance of the air, sea, and land are all parts of America's power, but what Paine wrote about the navy and geopolitical reality remains as true now as it was then.

An army of principles will penetrate where an army of
soldiers cannot;

It will succeed where diplomatic management would fail:
It is neither the Rhine, the Channel, nor the ocean
That can arrest its progress: it will march
On the horizon of the world, and it will conquer.

AJ-344

"The times that tried men's souls," are over—
And the greatest and completest revolution the world
Ever knew, gloriously and happily accomplished. . . .
To see it in our power to make a world happy—
To teach mankind the art of being so—to exhibit,
On the theatre of the universe a character hitherto
unknown—
And to have, as it were, a new creation intrusted to our
hands,
Are honours that command reflection, and can
Neither be too highly estimated, nor too gratefully received.

AC-XIII-348

On these grounds I rest the matter.
And as no offer hath yet been made to refute
The doctrine contained in the former editions of this
pamphlet,
It is a negative proof, that either the doctrine cannot be
refuted,
Or, that the party in favour of it are too numerous to be
opposed.
Wherefore, instead of gazing at each other with suspicious
Or doubtful curiosity, let each of us, hold out to his
neighbour
The hearty hand of friendship, and unite in drawing a
line,
Which, . . . shall bury in forgetfulness every former
dissention.

The concept of human freedom is indivisible. It is not merely the cause of a few men, long ago. It is not by accident the students in Tiananmen Square used the words of Jefferson and a replica of the Statue of Liberty to state their cause against the dictators of China. Their sense of freedom was no different from that which Paine inspired in the hearts of

America two centuries ago. But since then, history has taught a harsh lesson: as hard as it is to gain freedom from dictators, it is harder still to maintain that freedom, to raise up citizens worthy of freedom, to create structures of government and society that will defend freedom rather than erode it away. Both of these lessons were taught by Paine. Peoples around the world need to grasp them both. And Americans, in the land that gave birth to these, need to learn them again, lest they be forgotten, and, being forgotten, be lost to us.

Let the names of Whig and Tory be extinct;
And let none other be heard among us,
Than those of a good citizen, an open and resolute friend,
And a virtuous supporter of the rights of mankind
And of the free and independent States of America.
CS-Appendix-54

The American CRISIS

The Style and Success of Paine's Works

COMMON SENSE is the most successful book ever published in the United States. When Paine published it in 1776, the nation's population was under three million. Of those people, only one-third were literate.

The total sales of *Common Sense* were about 500,000 copies, or one for every two Americans who could read. Because printers simply took copies of *Common Sense*, set new type, and then sold copies without informing Paine, an accurate number of copies sold is impossible to obtain. I have seen figures as low as 400,000 and as high as 600,000. The number used here is simply the average between those two.

Now, there are slightly more than 300 million Americans. About 200 million adults can read and write. That means a modern book, to match *Common Sense*, would have to sell about 100 million copies. No other book, except the Bible, has sold copies equal to that proportion of the literate adult population at any time in American history.

In modern context, the sales of *Common Sense* exceeded even the sales of the most popular records, tapes, and even movie tickets bought, for the most popular of these ever produced. And these appeal to a much larger market; literacy is unnecessary to enjoy films or tapes. Though this seems a trivial comparison, it is true that a larger proportion of Americans bought and read the works of Paine in his day than bought any song by the Beatles today or bought tickets to any *Star Wars* movie. Paine's works became part of American culture to a greater extent than the works of anyone else in any medium at any time in history.

Paine himself thought that 100,000 copies of *Common Sense* were sold in 1776. Total sales of this book can only be estimated because many publishers, unconnected with Paine, published their own editions of this work. In Paine's era, there were no "copyrights." Anyone with a press in England or America could and did typeset and publish their own editions of any popular book. The author received no royalties from that.

Though the U.S. Constitution as a whole was a new creation, it has only one provision not found in prior governments or theory. The one clause with no precedent was patents and copyrights. It was invented by Benjamin Franklin to deal with the wholesale loss of the value of created works to writers and inventors in America and Europe. A prime example that led Franklin to propose this clause was the experience of his protege, Tom Paine, in the nationwide copying of his work *Common Sense.*

Franklin saw the same expropriation of the creations of scientists and inventors. Paine was one of these as well. His design of an iron bridge became the standard for construction of such bridges until better materials than iron were developed. Paine earned nothing from this, either. Franklin's design of patent protection was intended to cure both of these problems.

About twenty editions of *Common Sense* were published, most without Paine's knowledge. Even those that he did authorize were published without royalties. All were published anonymously, since his attacks on King George III were clearly treasonous and constituted a hanging offense if Paine had ever been proven to be the author. So the name attached to the book was simply this: *Common Sense.*

After the publication of *Common Sense*, Paine continued to write on the subject of American independence and the progress of the war. He published *The American Crisis* as a series of thirteen newspaper articles, afterward collected and published in book form.

All his life, Paine stayed with the themes of government, society, and the nature of man. The time line on page 227 shows his principal works in parallel with the events he observed and took part in in the

United States and in France. The quotations in this book are drawn from his entire opera.

The success of *Common Sense* and Paine's other works did not depend solely on selling copies to be read. His words also reached those Americans who could not read. His writings were read aloud in taverns and other public places so those who could not read them could hear them.

The style of Paine's writing contributed to his success. He wrote not just for the mind, but for the ear. The finest book on the subject of writing is *The Elements of Style* by Strunk and White. Everyone who writes should own and on occasion reread this text on the basics of writing English. In its final chapter, also titled "The Elements of Style," Strunk and White discuss the difference between writing that is merely competent and that which is excellent.

As Strunk and White say in their original editions, the final step to writing that "sings" is crafting sentences that are perfectly formed; sentences that not only speak clearly, but are incapable of being improved by any change. The example they chose to prove the point was the first line of *The American Crisis* by Paine:

> These are the times that try men's souls.

They rewrite this sentence four times and each change keeps the meaning but damages the "sound" and "feel" of the words. The worst style, which grates on the ear compared to Paine's original, is advertising:

> Soulwise, these are trying times.

It is not by accident that Paine wrote with the excellence he displayed, which prompted this book to showcase that quality of his work. Although Paine left school at twelve, he was already introduced to the classics. He knew the works of Shakespeare and Pope, and of Homer, Ovid, Cervantes, and others. Most of all, he knew and had an ear for the "heroic measure," now called iambic pentameter.

Consider how Homer's *The Iliad* and *The Odyssey* connect directly with the way *Common Sense* was communicated to most Americans. For perhaps two centuries after their creation, Homer's epic poems were not written down. They were recited to audiences from memory. For the texts to survive for generations in that form, they had to be memorable, clear, and powerful. They were "written for the ear," as Strunk and White now advise. The same tradition of oral preservation of the classics yet survives in some parts of Africa and Asia.

Paine recognized the power of poetry. He understood that it is not a matter of rhyme, but is a matter of style and rhythm. He was right; words written in "heroic measure" are more memorable and communicate better, not just then but for all time.

The classic "heroic measure" is ten syllables, five hard accents, five soft accents. If written in pure iambic pentameter: "The mass of men lead lives of qui [et] desper [ation]" (the syllables in brackets break the pattern in this famous quote by Henry David Thoreau). A long text written entirely this way would be offensive, not attractive, to the ear. It would have all the appeal of listening to a metronome. Homer, Ovid, Shakespeare, Pope, and Paine all realized that variations were needed to make it work.

The lines can have extra soft syllables or the hard syllables can be differently placed. The lines become more powerful to the extent that the soft syllables are eliminated and all that remains are the hard syllables.

Consider these examples of heroic measure from sources both ancient and modern:

From the Bible, King James Version:

"The Lord is my shepherd; I shall not want."

—Psalms 23:1

". . . The love of money is the root of all evil."

—1 Timothy 6:10

> "Forgive us our debts as we forgive our debtors,
> And lead us not into temptation,
> But deliver us from evil,
> For Thine is the Kingdom, and
> The Power, and the Glory forever."
>
> —Matthew 6:12–13

From Shakespeare:

> "To be, or not to be: that is the question."
>
> —*Hamlet* (3.1)

> "This above all: to thine own self be true,
> And it must follow, as the night the day,
> Thou canst not then be false to any man."
>
> —*Hamlet* (1.3)

> "Now is the winter of our discontent,
> Made glorious summer by this sun of York."
>
> —*Richard III* (1.1)

> "I come to bury Caesar, not to praise him."
>
> —*Julius Caesar* (3.2)

> "What's in a name? that which we call a rose
> By any other name would smell as sweet."
>
> —*Romeo and Juliet* (2.2)

> "Shall I compare thee to a summer's day?"
>
> —Sonnet 18

From Alexander Pope:

> "A little Learning is a dang'rous Thing;
> Drink deep, or taste not the Pierian Spring."
> —*An Essay on Criticism*

> "Fools rush in where angels fear to tread."
> —*An Essay on Criticism*

> "To err is human, to forgive, divine."
> —*An Essay on Criticism*

> "Hope springs eternal in the human breast. . . ."
> —*An Essay on Man* (I)

From Miguel Cervantes:

> "Let us make hay while the sun shines."
> —*Don Quixote* (I:3.11)

> "A bird in the hand is worth two in the bush."
> —*Don Quixote* (I:4.4)

> "Let every man look before he leaps."
> —*Don Quixote* (II:14)

> "The proof of the pudding is the eating."
> —*Don Quixote* (II:24)

From international writers:

> "No man is an island entire of itself;
> Every man is a piece of the Continent, a part of the main. . . .
> Any man's death diminishes me

Because I am involved in Mankind;
And therefore never send to know
For whom the bell tolls; it tolls for thee."
—John Donne, *Devotions Upon Emergent Occasions*

"How do I love thee?
Let me count the ways."
—Elizabeth Barrett Browning,
Sonnets from the Portuguese (XLIII)

". . . Humanity will proclaim by the lips of their sages
That there is no crime, and therefore no sin;
There is only hunger? 'Feed men,
And then ask of them virtue!'"
—Fyodor Dostoevsky, *The Brothers Karamazov* (V:5)

"The proletarians have nothing to lose but their chains. . . .
Working men of all countries, unite!"
—Karl Marx, *Manifesto of the Communist Party*

From the Statue of Liberty:

". . . Give me your tired, your poor,
Your huddled masses yearning to breathe free,
The wretched refuse of your teeming shore,
Send these, the homeless, tempest-tossed to me,
I lift my lamp beside the golden door!"
—Emma Lazarus, "The New Colossus"

From founding documents of the United States:

"Men are endowed by their Creator
With certain unalienable rights—
That among these are life, liberty and the pursuit of happiness."
—the Declaration of Independence

". . . for the support of this Declaration, with a firm reliance
On the protection of divine Providence,
We mutually pledge to each other
Our Lives, our Fortunes and our sacred Honor."
—the Declaration of Independence

"We the People of the United States,
In order to form a more perfect Union,
Establish Justice, insure domestic Tranquility,
Provide for the common Defence, promote the general Welfare,
And secure the Blessings of Liberty to ourselves and our posterity,
Do ordain and establish this Constitution
For the United States of America."
—Preamble, United States Constitution

From presidential speeches:

"The Constitution, unless changed
By the authentic act of the whole people,
Is sacredly obligatory upon all."
—George Washington, "Farewell Address"

"We are all Republicans, we are all Federalists.
If there be any among us who would wish
To dissolve this Union or to change its republican form,
Let them stand undisturbed as monuments of the safety
With which error of opinion may be tolerated
Where reason is left free to combat it."
—Thomas Jefferson, "First Inaugural Address"

"So that government of the people, by the people, for the people
Shall not perish from the Earth."
—Abraham Lincoln, "Gettysburg Address"

"The credit belongs to the man who is actually in the arena,
Whose face is marred by dust and sweat and blood;
Who strives valiantly; who errs, and comes short again and again,
Because there is no effort without error and shortcoming;
But who does actually strive to do the deeds . . . "

—Theodore Roosevelt, "Citizenship in a Republic," speech to the faculty of the Sorbonne in 1910

"Ask not what your country can do for you,
Ask what you can do for your country."

—John F. Kennedy, "Inaugural Address"

". . . an historian later said, [of Sir Francis Drake]
'He lived by the sea, died on it, and was buried in it.'
Well, today we can say of the Challenger crew:
Their dedication was, like Drake's, complete."

—Ronald Reagan, speech on the shuttle *Challenger*

"Mr. Gorbachev, tear down this wall."

—Ronald Reagan, speech at the Berlin Wall

From American literature:

"The difference between the right word and the almost right word
is a really large matter—it's the difference
between the lightning bug and the lightning."

—Mark Twain, printed in the National Endowment for the Arts edition of *Tom Sawyer*

"Those who cannot remember the past are condemned to repeat it."

—George Santayana, *Life of Reason, Reason in Common Sense*, 1905

"There's a sucker born every minute."
—P. T. Barnum, attributed

From movies:

"Why don't you come up and see me, sometime?"
—W. C. Fields in *My Little Chickadee*

"Fasten your seatbelts. It's going to be a bumpy night."
—Bette Davis in *All About Eve*

"If you don't go with Laslo, you'll regret it.
Maybe not today, maybe not tomorrow, but someday
And for the rest of your life."
—Humphrey Bogart in *Casablanca*

"How does a girl like you get to be a girl like you?"
—Cary Grant in *North by Northwest*

"What we have here is a failure of communication."
—Strother Martin in *Cool Hand Luke*

"I believe in the sweet spot,
soft-core pornography, opening your presents
Christmas morning rather than Christmas Eve,
and I believe in long, slow, deep,
soft, wet kisses that last three days."
—Kevin Costner in *Bull Durham*

"A long time ago in a galaxy far, far away . . ."
—Opening words on screen, *Star Wars I*

"With great power comes great responsibility."
—Cliff Robertson in *Spider Man*

From songs:

> "You do that voodoo that you do so well"
> —Cole Porter, "You Do Something to Me"

> "You got trouble, right here in River City,
> With a capital T and that rhymes with P
> And that stands for pool."
> —Robert Preston, *The Music Man*

> "I'm crazy for trying, and crazy for loving you."
> —Patsy Cline, "Crazy"

> "How come your dog don't bite nobody but me?"
> —Mel Tillis, in the song by that name

> "Yesterday, all my troubles seemed so far away . . ."
> —the Beatles, "Yesterday"

> "But when I get home to you
> I find the things that you do,
> Will make me feel all right."
> —the Beatles, "A Hard Day's Night"

> "I'm not the man they think I am at all . . ."
> —Elton John, "Rocket Man"

> "Springtime for Hitler and Germany,
> Winter for Poland and France . . .
> The thing you've gotta know is,
> Everything is show biz . . .
> Heil myself, watch my show;
> I'm the German Ethel Merman don't you know?"
> —Mel Brooks, "Springtime for Hitler"

The example best known to all Americans is both poetry and heroic measure, though most don't recognize those qualities:

> "O, say can you see,
> By the dawn's early light,
> What so proudly we hailed,
> At the twilight's last gleaming. . . ."
>
> —Francis Scott Key,
> "The Star-Spangled Banner"

This powerful and memorable form of writing even finds its way into sports writing:

> "When the Great Scorer comes
> To mark against your name,
> He'll write not 'won' or 'lost'
> But how you played the game."
>
> —Grantland Rice, in *Time* magazine,
> "Evangelist of Fun," July 26, 1954

Forgive the use of so many examples. It is important to show that poetry is not dead in the English language today. The writing and reading of poetry as such may be restricted to English majors in college and moonstruck female teenagers, but poetry itself is alive and well. Find one child over the age of six who has not memorized "the words to at least a million tunes" and the point will be conceded that poetry is dead.

The persistence of the heroic measure is a matter of both sound and memory. Consider the humble telephone number. Long after exchanges like "Pennsylvania 6–5000" have gone the way of the dodo, we still write phone numbers as three digits, then four. We do this because the human mind can remember a group of three plus a group of four better than it can recall one group of seven. Why this is true is beyond the scope of this chapter, but it is undeniably so.

The heroic measure survives in our memories because it works. It survives in speeches, songs, and texts because good writers have an ear for it.

As this book demonstrates, Paine was ahead of his time. Like Thomas Jefferson, he was a renaissance man with interests across the span of human knowledge. When the text of the proposed new constitution crossed the Atlantic to Paris, it was debated in a group of three—Jefferson, Lafayette, and Paine.

Paine could see the future of America, beginning with the fact that America could and should exist. To the task of convincing Americans of their destiny he brought a self-taught, brilliant knowledge of English. We sometimes forget that Shakespeare wrote for the masses. It was the ordinary people of London, not kings and queens, who made his works successful. The same is true of Paine. Though he was a genius at the crafting of words, his success came because ordinary Americans responded to his words with their "lives, fortunes, and sacred honor."

Those who read his words, and the many more who heard them, were as unaware of his craft as Shakespeare's audiences. Paine's critical importance in American history is not in the art of his words, but in the results of them.

Paine believed absolutely in the power of reason. He was a man of the Enlightenment, at the very beginning of that era. It was his application of that reason to the Bible, and to Christianity itself, which alienated him from most of his colleagues from the Revolutionary era. He wrote at length that the Bible was false.

Like Thomas Jefferson, Albert Einstein, and many great thinkers in American history, Paine was a deist. He saw the intricate majesty of the universe and concluded that such a reality could not exist without a Creator to put it in motion. But in his rejection of all creeds, including Christianity, he became an alien in the nation he helped create.

The themes that Paine addressed all his life—the nature of government, of man, of tyranny—are forgotten in times of peace and plenty. It is only in times of crisis, when America is threatened, that we turn again to these fundamental questions.

The government and society of this nation are not based on mere mechanics and organization. The very reason that our constitution has outlived the constitutions of all other governments in history is that our institutions are based on the reality of man. Unlike so many other governments and societies, ours account for the freedom of human beings. Ours encourage the good of which we are capable, but also restrain the evil likewise in our nature.

Paine understood all this before America was born. He wrote it out in words of power and memory. Because the nature of man for good or evil has not changed since shots were fired on Lexington Green, the nature of our response to any national crisis has not changed either in the centuries that have passed since the "shot heard 'round the world."

From a would-be nation of three million souls huddled against the Atlantic coast of a mostly empty land, from farmers, hunters, shopkeepers, and sailors, we have grown to the largest, most advanced economy in the world—and the greatest political power. But as Paine recognized, such factors are not the most important ones. Only as long as we continue to recognize what America is and who we are as Americans, only so long will we be able to keep and enjoy our heritage.

In this sense, every crisis that America has ever faced, and every one it will face in the future, is the same. If we understand the nature of ourselves and our nation and commit ourselves to their protection, we will survive. If and when we confront a crisis and cannot do that, this American experiment in self-government will be over.

General Washington Enters Trenton
26 December, 1776

The Life and Times of Paine

Editor's Note: Some of these entries are based on the chronology found here: http://www.thomaspainefriends.org/paine-chronology.htm. However, errors made on that website have been corrected. Paine's publications are in bold. Historical events in England, America, and France are indicated by E, A, and F, respectively.

1721 E: Robert Walpole, successful politician and businessman, becomes the first "prime minister" and remains in office for almost twenty-one years, under two kings. He makes mercantilism and empire the two foci of the recently established United Kingdom.

1737: Pain(e) born January 29 in Thetford, Norfolk, England.

1750: Paine leaves school, apprenticed to father as a stay-maker.

1754 A: Hostilities between the English and French in Europe become active warfare in the American colonies as the French and Indian War begins, then-Colonel George Washington leads a British attack on Fort Duquesne, the French are victorious.

1754 A: The first meeting of representatives of the American colonies meet in Albany, New York, in the Albany Congress.

1755 A: British General Braddock is killed during the retreat from Duquesne, Washington successfully leads the perilous retreat.

1756 E: William Pitt becomes prime minister of England.

1757: Paine becomes stay-maker in London, attends scientific lectures on astronomy.

1759: Paine becomes master stay-maker in Sandwich, Kent. Marries Mary Lambert, who dies a year later.

1762: Paine becomes officer of excise service.

1763 E, A, F: The French and Indian War ends with the Treaty of Paris.

1765: Paine dismissed from excise service.

1765 E: British Parliament passes the Stamp Act.

1765 A: Patrick Henry delivers "Give me liberty or give me death" speech in the Virginia General Assembly.

1766: Paine teaches English at a private academy.

1768: Paine reappointed to excise service.

1770 A: Boston adopts the Non-Importation Agreement, Boston Massacre takes place.

1771: Paine marries Elizabeth Ollive.

1772: Paine publishes first major pamphlet, ***Case of the Officers of Excise***.

1773 E, A: England passes the Tea Act, Sons of Liberty respond with the Boston Tea Party.

1774: Paine discharged from excise service, again, separates from wife, comes to America with a letter of introduction from Ben Franklin, life saved by Dr. John Kearsley when he reaches Philadelphia with a serious illness, changes the spelling of his last name from Pain to Paine.

1774 E: England passes the Intolerable Acts to punish the people of Boston.

1774 A: The first Continental Congress meets in Philadelphia.

1775 A: Paine becomes editor of *The Pennsylvania Magazine*, anonymously publishes ***African Slavery in America***.

1775 A: Paul Revere and William Dawes warn the people of Massachusetts that the British are leaving Boston to raid the military stores at Concord and Lexington, the "shot heard 'round the world" is fired, General Washington named commander in chief.

1775 A: Colonial war ships set out to sea with the Gadsden Flag, bearing a rattlesnake and the slogan, "Don't tread on me."

1776 A: Paine enlists as aide de camp to General Nathanael Greene and publishes ***The Forester's Letters***.

1776 A: Paine publishes ***Common Sense***.

1776 A: Including pirated copies printed without Paine's knowledge, ***Common Sense*** became the most successful book in America (other than the Bible), selling almost as many copies as Americans who could read, the two-thirds who were not literate heard it read aloud in public places.

1776 A: Declaration of Independence passed by Congress on July 2 (that is not a misprint).

1776 A: General Washington defeated heavily in the Battle of Manhattan, narrowly escapes from New York and begins a retreat down the length of New Jersey under constant attack.

1776 A: Betsy Ross sews the first "American" flag with thirteen red and white stripes and thirteen stars on a blue field, the Continental Congress adopts it as the official United States flag the following year.

1776 A: Paine sent by General Washington to Philadelphia to complete and publish ***The American Crisis I***, copies are returned and read to Washington's remaining 2,000 able troops just before they crossed the Delaware at night, in a snowstorm to defeat the Hessians at Trenton, New Jersey, on December 26.

1777: Paine publishes ***Crisis II***, ***Crisis III***, and ***Crisis IV***, appointed by Congress as secretary to the Committee on Foreign Affairs.

1777 A: General "Gentleman Johnny" Burgoyne defeated and captured with his entire army at Saratoga, New York, due to an heroic charge by American General Benedict Arnold, who attacked and broke the center of the British lines.

1778: Paine publishes ***Crisis V***, ***VI***, and ***Crisis VII***.

1779: Paine resigns as foreign secretary as result of the Silas Deane affair (Paine later exonerated), appointed clerk of Pennsylvania Assembly.

1779 A: Captain John Paul Jones ("I have not yet begun to fight") defeats and captures the British ship *Serapis*, as his ship, the *Bonhomme Richard*, is sinking under him.

1780: Paine publishes ***Crisis VIII***, ***IX***, ***Crisis Extraordinary***, and ***Public Good***, receives honorary degree from University of Pennsylvania.

1780 A: Benedict Arnold's plot to betray West Point to the British is discovered and prevented.

1781: Paine accompanies Colonel John Laurens to France on a diplomatic mission.

1781 A: Articles of Confederation finally ratified.

1781 A: General Greene fights a series of running battles against General Cornwallis across South and North Carolina, eventually driving Cornwallis to Yorktown. In the meantime, the French fleet, under Admiral de Grasse, drives the British from the Chesapeake Bay. Bereft of naval support, Cornwallis surrenders his army at Yorktown, Virginia.

1782: Paine publishes ***Crisis X***, ***XI***, ***XII***, ***Supernumerary Crisis***, and ***Letter to Abbe Raynal***.

1783: Paine publishes ***Crisis XIII***.

1783 A, E: The United States and Great Britain sign the Treaty of Paris, officially ending the American Revolution. George Washington resigns his commission as general of the armies.

1784: New York State presents Paine with a farm at New Rochelle for his services to the cause of independence.

1785: Paine designs a single-arch iron bridge which remained the standard design into the twentieth century. He never earned any money for this invention.

1786: Paine publishes ***Dissertation on Government***, ***The Affairs of the Bank***, and ***Paper Money***.

1787: Paine takes bridge proposal to France to the Academy of Sciences, publishes ***Prospects on the Rubicon***.

1787 A: Answering the invitation of the Annapolis Convention of 1786, twelve states meet in Philadelphia to write and propose the Constitution.

1788: Paine returns to England to promote his bridge, visits parents, meets with notables including Edmund Burke.

1789 A: Constitution adopted when New Hampshire becomes the ninth state to ratify it.

1789 F: Estates General is called, the Commons refuses to report as a separate chamber, some members of the First Estate (clergy) join the Third, they call themselves a National Assembly and take the oath not to disband until a constitution is established, the Second Estate (nobility) joins in, the Bastille is stormed and taken.

1790 F: The French Assembly continues to act as a legislature, abolishes nobility, creates a currency, divides France and Paris into districts, the king is confined to Paris.

1790: Paine is given the key to the Bastille by the Marquis de Lafayette to present to George Washington.

1791 F: King attempts to flee, is captured.

1791: Paine publishes ***The Rights of Man*, *Part 1***, and ***A Republican Manifesto***.

1792 F: The Legislative Assembly is replaced by the new National Convention.

1792: Paine publishes ***The Rights of Man*, *Part 2***, and ***Letter Addressed to the Addressers***. He returns to France and is elected to the French Assembly from Calais, becoming one of the principal authors of the Constitution for the Republic of France.

1793 F: The Committee of Public Safety begins the government by terror.

1793: As a member of the National Assembly, Paine urges banishment, not execution, for Louis XVI and his family. Writes ***The Age of Reason*, *Part 1***. Expelled from the Assembly, imprisoned in the Luxembourg prison, death warrant issued by Robespierre.

1794: Both of Paine's cell mates are guillotined. He is spared by Robespierre's arrest and later death, writes ***The Age of Reason, Part 2***. The good offices of the new ambassador to France, James Monroe, may have aided Paine's release.

1794: Paine returns to the National Assembly, becomes known as "the republican" among Irish, English, and other revolutionaries then in France.

1795: Paine publishes ***Dissertation on the First Principles of Government***.

1797: Paine publishes ***Agrarian Justice***.

1800: Paine publishes ***Maritime Compact***, suggesting an association of nations which would remain neutral in the event of war among other nations.

1802 F: The French Revolution ends when Napoleon Bonaparte purges the Tribunate and the Legislative Body of his opponents and becomes dictator of France under its new constitution.

1802: Paine returns to America, lives off and on in New Rochelle and New York City.

1804: Paine publishes ***To the French Inhabitants of Louisiana***, rebuking them for seeking to continue the slave trade in the Louisiana Territory.

1806: Paine moves to New York City permanently after officials in New Rochelle deny him the right to vote because he had served in the French Assembly.

1809: Paine dies in New York on June 8, buried at his farm in New Rochelle.

1819: William Cobbett, an English democrat, removes Paine's remains from his grave and takes them to England, intending a "fitting burial" there and to use Paine's reburial as an aid to his workers movement in England. The scheme was not carried out and Cobbett's descendants lost Paine's remains.

Bibliography

Beck, Glenn. *Glenn Beck's Common Sense.* New York: Simon and Schuster, 2009.

Fast, Howard. *Citizen Tom Paine.* New York: Grove Atlantic, 1943.

Forstchen, William, and Newt Gingrich. *To Try Men's Souls.* New York: St. Martin's Press, 2009.

Kaye, Harvey J. *Thomas Paine and the Promise of America.* New York: Hill and Wang, 2005.

McCullough, David. *1776.* New York: Simon and Schuster, 2005.

Melton, Buckner F., Jr. *The Quotable Founding Fathers.* Dulles, VA: Potomac Books, 2004.

Paine, Thomas. *Common Sense and other Writings.* Edited by Joyce Appleby. New York: Barnes & Noble Classics, 2005.

Paine, Thomas. *Rights of Man.* New York: Cosimo Books, 2008.

Paine, Thomas. *Thomas Paine, Collected Writings.* Edited by Eric Foner. New York: Library of America, 1995.

INTERNET SOURCES

The Amazon page on Thomas Paine is here:
www.Amazon.com/Thomas-Paine/e/B000APJOHK

For a variety of websites dedicated to Paine and his works, see also:
http://www.thomaspainefriends.org/links.htm

Table of Citations

NOTE: Numbers after the letters indicate volume, if more than one, then chapter, then page. Unless otherwise indicated, the selections below are taken from Eric Foner's *Thomas Paine, Collected Writings.*

AC = *The American Crisis*
Adams-Letters = *To Samuel Adams*
AFA = *African Slavery in America,* in Appleby
AJ = *Agrarian Justice,* in Appleby
APA = *Appeal to Pennsylvania*
AR = *The Age of Reason*
ARep = *To the Authors of the Republican*
COB = *Construction of Iron Bridge*
CS = *Common Sense,* in Beck, except for exerpts from the appendix and post script, which come from Foner's *Collected Writings*
CSFW = *Common Sense on Financing the War*
CSQ = *To the Quakers of Philadelphia*
D = *To Danton*
FL = *Forester's Letters*
GC = *To Sir Guy Carleton*
GW = *To George Washington*
LP = *On the Term "Liberty of the Press"*
PG = *Public Good*
PLLC = *Preserving the Life of Louis Capet*
PM = *Paper Money*
RM = *The Rights of Man*
RMF = *The Rights of Man,* French edition published by Cosimo

Index

C

T

U

V

W

CPSIA information can be obtained at www.ICGtesting.com
Printed in the USA
LVOW07s0420241214

420180LV00002B/10/P

9 781457 535147